Presidential Playbook 2020

16 Nonpartisan Solutions to Save America

John Burke

LITTLE CREEK PRESS®
AND BOOK DESIGN

Mineral Point, Wisconsin

Little Creek Press®
A Division of Kristin Mitchell Design, Inc.
5341 Sunny Ridge Road
Mineral Point, Wisconsin 53565

Book Design and Project Coordination:
Little Creek Press

Editor: Judy Newman

First Edition
May 2020

Printed in the United States of America

For more information or to order books:
visit www.littlecreekpress.com;
www.PresidentialPlaybook.com
or email John Burke at john@presidentialplaybook.com

Library of Congress Control Number: 2020902280

ISBN-13: 978-1-942586-74-6

Data current as of March 31, 2020.

Table of Contents

Acknowledgments

Thank you to everyone who contributed to this book. I have had some great helpers along the way. I want to thank my old college roommate Mark Murphy who went through the manuscript many times and provided exceptional feedback. I want to thank a number of people at Trek—Pat Sullivan, Mark Joslyn, Chad Brown, Dr. Mark Timmerman, Bob Burns, and Roger Gierhart—who gave candid feedback along the way. I want to thank my high school basketball coach, Eric Walter, who has taught me many life lessons and continued to do so while I was writing this book. I want to thank Judy Newman for editing the book, and for doing some of the research. Judy was timely, organized, and provided great insight. Many thanks to Kristin Mitchell from Little Creek Press. Kristin brought the book to life with an excellent layout. My CEO (Chief Empathy Officer) is my assistant, Cindy Wagner. I have been lucky enough to work with Cindy for over 25 years and she helped read the draft a number of times and gave some great feedback, including the title of the book. A big thank you goes to my wife, Tania, who does an amazing job of reviewing my work and making it better—including this book. ✔

Foreword

I am not a politician. I am an avid observer of government and politics, and over the years, I have become extremely discouraged by the performance of our government and its refusal to tackle the serious issues facing our country and our world. I am also disgusted by the way we elect our political leaders, especially presidents.

The Democratic debate in Las Vegas in February 2020 was a prime example of what is wrong with our election process. Intelligent people who are applying for the most important job in the world behaved like eight-year-olds—yelling at each other, speaking out of turn, missing the facts left and right, accusing people of falsehoods, and worst of all, not having an honest and comprehensive plan for the job they are seeking. As Americans, we should be embarrassed by our current political process. We deserve better.

I am an optimist. When I see a problem, I want to solve it. After the 2016 election, I vowed that if someone competent did not run for president in 2020 with a comprehensive plan for our nation, I would run for president myself.

In 2018, I began writing a book which would define my plan for the nation. When I finished the book, I faced the question: Should I carry through with my intent and run for president?

In the end, I came to the conclusion that I would not run for the presidency for the following reasons:

1. The chances of winning were very low. After discussing a potential campaign with a number of people, I came to the conclusion that running for president as an Independent would be very difficult. I like to play games that I have a chance to win.

2. I would not be a good fundraiser. One of the biggest problems we have in this country is money in politics. In order to be competitive, I would have had to raise a significant amount of money.

3. As I finished writing this book, I came to the conclusion that my greatest contribution to the country would be to educate the American people on the major issues our nation faces.

So, I am presenting the exact book that I would have published if I had run for president. Here's why:

• The vast majority of Americans know very little about the current problems we face as a country. This book offers an opportunity for citizens to become educated on the most critical issues, along with nonpartisan solutions for 16 of our biggest challenges.

• The political conversation in our country has become an argument between two "warring tribes" with very few facts. My plan is based on FACTS, and it is nonpartisan. Hopefully the FACTS can bring people together.

• No current candidate for the most important job in the world has presented a comprehensive plan that challenges the American people. I hope that by publishing this book, the candidates for president and for any public office in 2020 and beyond will choose to present the American people with a plan for the future based on facts and based on shared sacrifice. It is also my hope that after reading this book, both citizens and politicians will set their sights higher and will realize that as a nation, we have work to do.

I hope you will enjoy reading the book. Please pass it along to your friends. A free downloadable pdf is available at www.PresidentialPlaybook.com or in other digital formats online for a small fee. I want as many people as possible to know as much as possible about our country, the challenges we face, and the simple solutions that can help save America. A knowledgeable electorate is in everyone's best interest. ✔

Jb

> "And sometime, at some point,
> do something for your country."
>
> —David McCullough, Pulitzer Prize-winning historian[1]

Introduction

A t my son's graduation from Marquette University in 2011, the keynote speaker was David McCullough, a renowned historian and Pulitzer Prize-winning author whom I've long admired. Little did I imagine how much impact that commencement address would have—not just on the graduates, but on me. McCullough stressed the importance of reading. "We are what we read more than we realize, and notable readers are most notably leaders." It was a memorable message. But it was McCullough's final piece of advice that struck me deeply: "And sometime, at some point, do something for your country.

Over the years, I have become increasingly frustrated with the performance of our government. I see a great nation in decline, a nation that has done so much for so many, a nation with an incredible history and such amazing potential being wasted because the leaders of our country care more about their political careers and their pocketbooks than the state of the union. On the drive home to Madison that night, I thought about what McCullough said: "Do something for your country." What could my contribution be? I decided to write a short book in which I would propose simple solutions to what I see are the biggest problems in the United States.

In May 2016, I finished writing my book, *12 Simple Solutions to Save America.*[2] I laid out a simple, clear vision for the future of the country by addressing 12 of the biggest issues that we face as a nation, with specific recommendations on how to resolve each one. When the book was completed, I sent copies to Donald Trump, Hillary Clinton, President Obama, and to many other national leaders. I did my best to get the word out, to educate people on our biggest problems and how they could be solved. As I watched the 2016 election unfold, my opinion that our political system is broken and that

we need massive change in the country deepened. I listened to the candidates talk about everything except the major issues, and I witnessed the American public being dumbed down by billions of dollars' worth of negative advertising. When the election ended, I was disgusted. I didn't like the candidates, I didn't like the process, and I didn't like the outcome.

As an American, I am embarrassed at the current state of politics in our country. We used to be a shining city on a hill, the benchmark for free countries around the world to aspire to be. Now, all too often, we are a global embarrassment. According to a February 2019 Pew Research Center report, 45 percent of nations around the world see U.S. power and influence as a major threat, up from 25 percent in 2013,[3] while favorable views of the U.S. are at historic lows, according to a Gallup survey at the end of 2018.[4] Since President Trump's election, I have been concerned that in 2020, we would see a repeat of 2016: Major candidates raising hundreds of millions of dollars from supporters who expect a return on their investment; major candidates telling people whatever they want to hear to earn their votes; major candidates beating each other up and lying about their opponents' records because negative advertising wins.

After the 2016 election, I promised myself that for the 2020 campaign, if no candidate emerged who had a specific plan and the leadership skills to deliver the plan and bring the country together, I would run for president as an Independent. This book is my specific, bold plan for the United States, and I believe that I have the leadership skills to bring the country together and solve many of our nation's biggest problems.

I will run for president as an Independent who focuses on substance over style. I will ask people to put their country ahead of their interests. I will run a campaign that focuses on the facts. I will not participate in any negative campaigning, and I will treat the American people with the respect they deserve when they are making their decision about who should lead our country for the next four years.

I have been told by seasoned political professionals who have participated in successful presidential campaigns that the American people don't care about the real issues. I have been told by the experts that if I run a campaign for president with a simple, clear, bold plan based on the facts that I am doomed. To reinforce their point, they showed me a passage from the book, *All the King's Men*, written by Robert Penn Warren in 1946:

> Yeah, I said, I heard the speech. But they don't give a damn about that. Hell, make 'em cry, make 'em laugh, make 'em think you're their weak erring pal, or make 'em think you're God Almighty. Or make 'em mad. Even mad at you. Just stir 'em up, it doesn't matter how or why, and they'll love you and come back for more. Pinch 'em in the soft place. They aren't alive, most of 'em, and haven't been alive in twenty years. Hell, their wives have lost their teeth and their shape, and likker won't set on their stomachs, and

they don't believe in God, so it's up to you to give 'em something to stir 'em up and make 'em feel alive again. Just for half an hour. That's what they come for. Tell 'em anything. But for Sweet Jesus' sake don't try to improve their minds.[5]

I don't believe it. I think this attitude has transformed American elections into soap operas not only by failing to educate the public, but by spreading so much misinformation through negative advertising that no one knows what the real truth is. Without real knowledge, we make poor decisions. Without an educated citizenry, our democracy is at risk.

I have made my mark in life by listening to people and looking at every issue from all points of view, by respecting the facts, by searching out new ideas, by trying new things, by having faith in people and by being an optimist. I believe that our nation needs facts. I believe our nation needs a simple, bold plan for the future, and I believe I have the leadership skills to deliver on that plan. That is why I am running for president.

Why am I qualified to be president of the United States? Here are my top ten reasons:

1. I have a good moral compass. I have been lucky enough to have two amazing parents. They taught me the difference between right and wrong; they taught me the lesson of putting other people first; and they taught me that to whom much is given, much is required.

2. I am a good listener, and I ask a lot of questions. They say there are two types of people in the world: know-it-alls and learn-it-alls. I am a learn-it-all. I like to get the smartest people in a room, ask a lot of questions, write down what I hear on a whiteboard, and then make a decision. If elected president, I would put a whiteboard in the Oval Office.

3. I can see something bigger than the barn. My father started Trek in a small, red barn in Waterloo, Wisconsin. Some people saw a barn; he always saw something bigger. So do I. I take a look at every opportunity, every problem, every situation, and I always think outside the box. I try to see something bigger. Some people see a nation in trouble; I see a nation without a simple, clear, bold plan.

4. I have traveled the world. I have been to Europe more than 100 times. I have been to Asia more than 30 times. I have done business in over 100 countries. I have met people from around the world and have experienced many different cultures. As the world becomes smaller, having a global view is an asset.

5. I am an optimist. I look at the glass as being half-full, and I believe that all problems can be solved. We have some big problems in our country, and I see these problems as an incredible opportunity to make changes and move our country forward.

6. I have run a successful business with a great team of people. When I started at Trek Bicycle in 1984, sales were $20 million. In 2019, Trek did over $1.0 billion in sales in over 100 countries.

7. I can put together a great team. At Trek, the majority of the senior management team has been at Trek for over 20 years. Trek is certified as "A Great Place to Work" by the global business consultant Great Place to Work Institute. I have a track record of building a strong team, and I would put the best team on the field throughout the federal government.

8. I take full responsibility. In business, sports, and politics, you make some good decisions, and you make some bad ones. I have a sense of humility, and if my team makes a mistake, I take responsibility. I don't look to blame others. I learn from my mistakes and move on.

9. I can simplify things. I like to listen to all angles of an issue, and I am good at simplifying complex problems, making decisions and giving directions.

10. I have an amazing wife. Tania is smart, fun, great with people, a good listener, and has a strong sense of ethics. She would represent the country very well.

Today, our nation faces many complicated issues that present major problems: a national debt over $23 trillion;[6] a 2,652-page tax code that makes no sense;[7] a two degree increase in global temperature since the 1880s;[8] a legal system that is out of control; a Congress with a dismal approval rating,[9] and an election process that threatens our democracy, just to name a few.

Lincoln observed that the Constitution created a government "of the people, by the people, and for the people." It is time that "We, the people" stand up and take responsibility for our government.

I feel a debt to this country, and I believe that my contribution to our nation is addressing the challenges and opportunities that lie in front of us—running a good, clean campaign that Americans can be proud of and, if I am elected, providing the leadership to change the course of our nation for the better. We have real problems as a country that need to be addressed, and I believe I can offer the facts, creative solutions, and the leadership to move our country forward honestly and ethically.

As a candidate for president, I will be running a different type of campaign. Here is what you can expect from me:

1. A plan based on facts. For a very long time, presidential candidates have spent the majority of their time raising money and talking in broad generalities. Presidential candidates spend very little time talking in detail about their plans for the future of our country. Specifically, what would the candidate do to move our country forward? I cannot find one example of a presidential candidate in the last 50 years who has run for the highest office in the land with a real plan that challenges the American people.

I believe that success in any organization depends on two key components. The first is a solid plan. The second is a team of people who can execute the plan. I am running for president because I care about this country and because no other candidate has a comprehensive plan to move our country forward. This book constitutes my plan, if I am elected. It defines 16 of the toughest issues holding our nation back. For each issue, I lay out the facts and offer a simple, clear, bold plan.

Former Senator Daniel Patrick Moynihan of New York once said that "everyone is entitled to his own opinion, but not to his own facts."[10] Nebraska Senator Ben Sasse has said that "we have a risk of getting to a place where we don't have shared public facts.[11] A republic will not work if we don't have shared facts." As a nation, we have developed a bad habit of debating issues with little regard for the facts, and we have developed more loyalty to our political party than to our country. Many of the problems we face do not get solved because the majority of the country does not know the facts that surround the major issues that we face. Our political leaders spend very little time educating the public and proposing new ideas to address the problems.

Lincoln observed that the Constitution created a government **"of the people, by the people, and for the people."** It is time that **"We, the people" stand up and take responsibility for our government.**

My plan is bold, specific, detailed, and will ask a lot of the American people. You might not like all of it, but it is clear and straightforward, and it takes our most challenging problems out of the attic and puts them on the table. A presidential election should provide an opportunity for the American voter to interview the candidates, to know where the candidates stand on the major issues, and to know if the candidate is elected, what plan the candidate has to move the country forward. I will spend my time during the campaign sharing my plan with the American people. I am more concerned about being honest about our problems, with an intense focus on real solutions and our opportunities as a nation, than I am about getting elected.

2. I will challenge the American people. During the 1960 presidential campaign, John F. Kennedy said, in his speech accepting the Democratic nomination, "The New Frontier of which I speak is not a set of promises—it is a set of challenges. It sums up not what I intend to offer the American people, but what I intend to ask of them."[12] Traditional American political campaigns have turned into candidates falling over each other to offer voters treats—tax cuts when we are $23 trillion in debt, more defense spending when we spend more on defense than the next eight nations combined,[13] better roads with no plans on how to fund the roads at a time when the Highway Trust Fund is broke...[14] The list goes on and on.

My campaign will focus on our biggest challenges and what the American people can do to help solve them. I intend to talk honestly about these challenges, the opportunities they present, and how all Americans can make a difference.

The United States is a democracy, and that means at the end of the day, the people own the problems. The only way we can reach our potential as a nation is for everyone to pitch in.

3. I will run as an Independent. I believe the current party system in America is broken. I think the majority of politicians are good people, but they make decisions in the best interest of their party, not in the best interest of the country. A Gallup poll conducted in October 2019 showed that 26 percent of Americans identified themselves as Republicans, 29 percent as Democrats, and 43 percent as Independents.[15] I am an Independent because I have always voted independently. I vote for the person, not the party. Some of my positions can be considered liberal and some conservative. I will look at the facts behind every issue to make decisions in the best interest of the American people, not in the best interest of a political party.

4. I will run with humility. Our country has a great tradition of humble leaders—great people who put the success of our nation ahead of their personal success. People like presidents George Washington, Abraham Lincoln, Theodore Roosevelt, Franklin Roosevelt, Dwight Eisenhower, and Ronald Reagan. Eisenhower once wrote, "My own conviction is that every leader should have enough humility to accept, publicly, the responsibility for the mistakes of the subordinates he has himself selected and, likewise, to give them credit, publicly, for their triumphs."[16] I have spent my life living by these words, and if elected, I will continue to lead with a sense of humility.

5. I will run a positive campaign. I will not run negative ads about my opponents. My campaign will focus on my plan for America. I believe that presidential campaigns should be an interview for the American people. One of the problems we have as a country is the poor manners of our politicians. How can we expect people to treat each other well when we see our national leaders lying about each other and setting such a poor example of how we should treat others?

6. I will only accept campaign contributions from real people. That means I will take no contributions from political action committees, unions, or businesses. If I am elected, I will owe no one except the American people. My focus will be on making the best long-term decisions for the American people.

I believe that campaign contributions are one of the root causes of the current problems we face as a country. Our democracy is based on one person, one vote. Yet, the ability a single person or organization has to move an election by throwing a huge amount of money to a candidate is eroding people's faith in our democracy. The amount of money pouring into our political system is out of control. In 2016, candidates running for federal office spent a record $6.4 billion, while lobbyists spent $3.15 billion to influence the candidates whom they helped elect. Both amounts are twice what they were during the 2000 election, according to *The New York Times*.[17] When the 2020 election is over, I will owe no one except for my obligation to the American people who put me in office. If a candidate from a major party wins, he or she will have a very long list of people they owe and will pay them off with decisions that may not be in the best interest of the American people. My campaign will not accept any contribution over $2,800. If I am elected president, I will fill all jobs with the *best* available talent, and I will make decisions in the best interest of the American people, not campaign contributors. ✔

Core Beliefs

Over the past 30 years, many of our presidential candidates have run on a platform they like to call "American values." Almost always, the values that candidates talk about are poorly defined, and when they are defined, they typically focus on contentious social issues. All great sports teams, all great companies, and all great organizations have a core set of values that serve as a guide. The following core beliefs will guide my administration as we transform our nation:

 CORE BELIEF #1:
Deal with reality. Great leaders deal with reality.

Great organizations deal with reality. During World War II, President Franklin D. Roosevelt and British Prime Minister Winston Churchill dealt with reality. They clearly let the people know there would be tough times ahead, but that in the end, we would prevail. Churchill did not mince words. He let the people know the situation was grim, and they might need to fight the Germans on the beaches, and they might need to fight them in the streets, but they would prevail. Roosevelt did the same throughout the Great Depression and the war. He let Americans know the dire situation we faced, the sacrifices that needed to be made, and that we would prevail in the end. Contrast the way President Roosevelt truthfully told the grim reality of World War II to the American people with the way President Donald Trump has continually misled the public about the coronavirus pandemic.

In spite of early warnings about the disease from U.S. health officials and intelligence agencies,[1] and the first case of COVID-19 confirmed in the U.S. on Jan. 20, 2020,[2] two days later, Trump told a broadcast interviewer, "We have it totally under control … it's going to be just fine."[3]

On February 24, with 14 cases diagnosed in the U.S. and nearly 79,000 cases worldwide,[4] Trump tweeted, "The Coronavirus is very much under control in the USA.… Stock Market starting to look very good to me!"[5]

On March 10, with more than 113,000 cases and 4,000 deaths worldwide—including 712 COVID-19 cases and 27 deaths in the U.S.,[6] Trump said, "And it hit the world. And we're prepared, and we're doing a great job with it. And it will go away. Just stay calm. It will go away."[7]

COVID-19 is one of the greatest health crises to hit the United States. As your president, I will always deal with reality, and I will clearly and honestly communicate with the American people.

2 CORE BELIEF #2: Put everything on the table.
If I am elected your president, I will assemble a world-class team of people. We will put all of the nation's problems on the table. We will get the smartest people in the room from within the government and outside of government. Republicans, Democrats, and Independents will come up with solutions, however painful they might be, and take action with a sense of urgency.

We will instill the same sense of urgency that Steve Jobs had when he came back to run Apple in 1997 and took the company from near-bankruptcy to one of the most valuable companies in the world.[8] He put everything on the table, he questioned everything, and he moved quickly. My administration will do the same.

3 CORE BELIEF #3:
Shared sacrifice. Everyone needs to contribute.

"Ask not what your country can do for you; ask what you can do for your country." President John F. Kennedy spoke these words nearly 60 years ago.[9] He asked his fellow citizens to focus on the success of the nation first and on themselves second. Yet, what does our country look like today? For the most part, we ask: What can government do for *me*? Tax breaks, new programs. In two generations, we have transitioned from "The Greatest Generation" that focused on what we can do for our country to the "Me Generation" focused on what the government can do for me.

Today, as we tackle some of the greatest problems this nation has ever faced, I will make sure that I assemble a group of leaders who will put the nation first and their personal interests last.

It is important to understand that no one will ever agree with all of the decisions and policies that come from my administration. Likewise, you will not agree with every decision made at your company or in your family. It is better to be part of the effort in building something great than to spend time being bitter and tearing things apart because you disagree on a couple of issues. I will demand that my administration be open-minded to all points of view from all citizens, whether they are Democrats, Republicans, Independents, or none of the above. We all need to be Americans first.

If elected president, I will challenge the American people. Problems like the national debt, gun violence, and climate change are only getting worse with time. My administration will provide the leadership to solve these problems. I will be asking you to participate in your democracy with an open mind, focusing on the facts, and tackling solutions that are in the best interest of the entire country, not just one specific interest group.

We have an amazing opportunity to make a big difference in the future of our nation. After reading my previous book, someone told me something that I will never forget: "I have been a lifelong Republican. I read your book, and I agree with every single point. If you get smart people in a room and put all the facts on the table, more than 90 percent of people will come to the same conclusion."

I will provide the leadership to put the tough issues on the table, and I will make sure there is a diverse group of people in the room. I will be a very good listener, and at the end of the discussion, I will make sure that we have a simple, clear direction moving forward.

4 **CORE BELIEF #4:**
Ensure the U.S. government serves us, the people.

The U.S. Constitution says the power of government comes from "We, the people." Lincoln stated at Gettysburg that the government should be "of the people, by the people, and for the people."[10] If the government really is of the people, by the people, and for the people, then shouldn't the people be happy with the performance of our government? Shouldn't we strive to have the best-performing government in the world? A government with world-class service, world-class productivity, and incredible innovation in the workplace. We actually have that in the military. Think about the Marines or any of our special forces. They only recruit the best, they set high standards, and they hold people accountable.

This is similar to the way any world-class company works. Think of Apple or The Walt Disney Company. They hire the best, demand high-performance, and if you don't perform at a high level, you are gone. When it comes to the rest of the government, there is an entirely different attitude. Our government tends to be more interested in protecting the status quo and justifying poor performance than it is in putting the best team on the field and making sure that the products and services the government is delivering are the best possible.

To turn this country around, we need to start with the government. My administration will strive to build the most productive government in the world. To do that, we will fill the government with the best managers and the best employees, and we will make the U.S. government a great place to work. The U.S. government should be a government of the people, by the people, and for the people.

5 **CORE BELIEF #5: Simplify everything we do.**
Over time, our government has become too complicated. These are just a few examples:

- The Patient Protection and Affordable Care Act of 2010 increased the number of federally mandated categories of illness and injuries for which hospitals may claim reimbursement from 18,000 to 140,000.[11] Did you know that there are nine reimbursement codes related to injuries caused by parrots and three codes of injuries caused by flaming water skis?

- The U.S. tax code is 2,652 pages long.

- The General Accounting Office has found 903 examples of overlapping federal services or untapped revenues, amounting to hundreds of billions of dollars. In annual reports issued since 2011,[12] the GAO has called out duplicated efforts, including 159 contracts for foreign language support for the military that cost $1.2 billion more than the $5.2 billion already approved for those services; 45 programs across nine federal agencies to help people with disabilities to find jobs; 76 programs in 15 agencies aimed at preventing or treating drug abuse; and 679 renewable energy initiatives operated by 23 federal agencies in a single year.

The United States was founded and governed for more than two centuries based on a document that is six pages long, yet the current income tax code is more than 2,600 pages.[13] One of the great champions of simplicity in the 20th century was former Apple CEO Steve Jobs. Jobs believed that less is more and recognized that it takes hard work to make something simple. When Jobs was asked about the success of Apple, he explained, "The way we're running the company, the product design, the advertising—it all comes down to this: Let's make it simple. Really simple."[14]

My administration will work to simplify our government and all of its programs. We will work tirelessly to go through every government department and simplify our organizational structure. We will simplify the products and services that we offer. My administration will lead with simplicity in everything it does. ✔

16

Nonpartisan Solutions

What follows are my 16 nonpartisan solutions to maximize America's potential.

Implemented as soon as possible, my solutions would put this country back on the path to greatness, resulting in massive improvements throughout America, and would serve as an example to the rest of the world.

I will provide a clear choice for every American in the 2020 presidential election. Do citizens want more of the same or real change? And when I say real change, I mean being the first presidential candidate in a long time to have a bold, simple, clear plan for change. There have been many people who have run for the presidency on the theme of change. When they get elected, not much happens. I am running for president because I believe the United States needs real change, and I have the plan and the leadership skills to deliver it.

If I'm elected, my presidency will focus on the following key issues and solutions. This will be my task list as your president. I will work for you, and I will do all that I can to deliver on these key issues:

1. Demand a high-performance government. I will propose the *John McCain High-Performance Government Act of 2021*, where federal government employee unions are abolished, and the U.S. Labor Department will set the pay rates of all government jobs at the average rate of similar private-sector jobs. The citizens own the government, and we deserve a high-performance government. I will establish a simple, effective, annual evaluation process for all government employees, and my administration will remove all poor performers if they cannot meet the standards of the job. If you can't fire the players, you can never have a high-performing team. My administration will also make sure that the United States Government is a Great Place to Work.[1]

2. Address climate change with a sense of urgency. Ninety-seven percent of climate scientists believe that climate change is caused by humans burning fossil fuels, which in turn creates greenhouse gases that heat the planet.[2] It is my opinion that climate change is THE defining issue of our time and is currently having a massive impact on our land and our people. If we fail to act, the consequences in the years to come and to future generations could be catastrophic. If I am elected president, I will make sure the United States leads on this most important issue.

3. Reduce the risk of nuclear war. The United States has nearly 6,200 nuclear weapons. Of these, 1,750 are currently deployed.[3] The Department of Defense has a plan to spend $494 billion between 2019 and 2028 to modernize our nuclear fleet.[4] One of today's nuclear weapons has 1,000 times more destructive force than the bomb dropped on Hiroshima. As commander-in-chief, on my first day in office, I will cut the number of nuclear weapons deployed to around 300 to reduce the chances of a nuclear accident, and I will reduce by 80 percent the amount of money spent on nuclear weapons development in the future. We have more urgent needs as a nation than to spend $494 billion over the next 10 years on a weapon that should never be used.

4. Fix the health care system. We spend 17.7 percent of our gross domestic product on health care,[5] which is by far the highest in the world, yet our life expectancy doesn't even rank in the top 20 worldwide. We have the most expensive health care system in the world, and we get some of the worst results. I will propose the *Jack LaLanne Health Improvement Act of 2021*, where we will improve the health of our citizens, offer basic health insurance to every American, and significantly reduce our costs.

5. Rebuild America by increasing the gas tax. Our nation's infrastructure is rated a D+.[6] This is an embarrassment for the largest economy in the world. We have not raised the federal gas tax in more than 25 years. Meanwhile, with inflation raising costs for materials and labor and more people driving fuel-efficient cars, the buying power of gas tax revenues has been slashed by more than three-fourths.[7] I will propose the *Eisenhower Two Transportation Act of 2021*, a massive infrastructure program to rebuild our nation's transportation system. I will pay for this program by increasing the gas tax from 18.4 cents per gallon to $1 per gallon.

6. Increase opportunity for every American. The gap between the rich and the poor continues to widen. This is bad news for both the rich and the poor. Nearly 13 million kids live below the poverty line, potentially dooming them to a life of poverty, through no fault of their own.[8] I will launch the *War on Poverty Act of 2021*, where we specifically target children born into poverty. Money invested in this program will save our nation hundreds of billions of dollars over time as we create taxpayers for the future instead of citizens who cannot break out of the cycle of poverty and could wind up addicted to government support programs or destined for the prison system. I also support boosting the federal minimum wage to $15 an hour to help families earn their way out of poverty.

7. Reform Congress. I will propose the *Congressional Reform Act of 2021*, where we will work to install term limits, ask members to serve their country for free if they have a net worth over $10 million, end gerrymandering, and give the president a line-item veto.

8. Cut defense spending. Admiral Michael Mullen, former chairman of the Joint Chiefs of Staff, has called our national debt the greatest threat to our security.[9] We can no longer afford to spend $1 trillion a year on defense when we are $23 trillion in debt.[10] I will work with the Department of Defense and related agencies to reduce our spending to $750 billion a year within two years.

9. Build positive relationships around the world to make the United States more secure and prosperous. As the world becomes smaller through technology, we need to engage with other nations. In over 240 years as a country, the U.S. has done more to liberate people from tyranny and poverty than any country in history. We need to re-engage with the world and, as Teddy Roosevelt suggested, walk softly and carry a big stick.

10. Reduce gun deaths in America. More than 10,000 Americans are murdered every year as a result of gun violence; as many as 100,000 more Americans are wounded in gun incidents.[11] Not only are individuals destroyed by these senseless acts, so too are many families. I will announce a simple program to cut gun violence by 90 percent in one year. The program will include universal background checks, mandatory gun registration—just like for cars— along with the elimination of all assault rifles, submachine guns, and high-capacity ammunition magazines. Every other major country in the world has these laws on the books, and they have the results to prove their effectiveness.

11. Fix the legal system. Our nation is choking on our legal system. I will propose the *Warren Burger Judicial Reform Act of 2021*, which will reduce civil lawsuits by more than 50 percent. The *Warren Burger Judicial Reform Act of 2021* will also seek to reduce our nonviolent prison population. We have more jailed citizens than any other country in the world. In 1925, seventy-nine of every 100,000 U.S. residents were behind bars, and in 1975, we had 111 people locked up per 100,000 population. Today that number is over 655 per 100,000.[12] In Japan, Germany, and the United Kingdom, the number is less than 150 per 100,000.[13] We can significantly reduce our prison population, drive down our costs, and increase the number of taxpaying citizens.

12. Embrace the immigration advantage. Immigration is a tough issue that must be dealt with. Ronald Reagan took office with a refugee crisis on his hands, with people from Cuba, Vietnam, and Cambodia coming to America. With a sense of history and optimism in the future, Reagan said, "We shall seek new ways to integrate refugees into our society."[14]

We need to control our borders, but we also need to understand that we are a nation of immigrants, as symbolized by the Statue of Liberty that welcomes people to our land. Many great people want to call America home, and the majority of these people can make a real contribution, both economically and socially, to the United States. When it comes to immigration, my administration will propose the *Statue of Liberty Immigration Act of 2021*, where we vigorously protect our borders and allow immigrants to come to the United States if they will contribute to the country socially and economically. Undocumented immigrants currently working and living in the United States and contributing to the country will be allowed to apply for citizenship. If there are undocumented immigrants who are breaking the law, my administration will move quickly and forcefully to exit them from the United States with all legal means necessary.

13. Save Social Security. One of our all-time great government programs hangs by a thread. I will propose the *Franklin Roosevelt Social Security Act of 2021*, which will raise the full retirement age for Social Security from 66 to 70 by 2024, and I will scrap the cap that prevents our nation's highest earners from paying a penny of Social Security tax on any money they earn over $132,900. All Americans should pay 6.2 percent of all income into Social Security.

14. Simplify the tax code. In the first 100 days of my administration, I will propose the *Tax Simplification Act of 2021*. Our current federal tax code is over 2,600 pages long. I have a specific proposal to reduce the tax code to 10 pages. The result will be increased fairness and the elimination of wasted time and costs for every taxpaying citizen.

15. Reform campaign finance. I will propose to Congress the *Campaign Finance Reform Act of 2021*, where businesses, unions, and PACs are prohibited from making campaign contributions. We need to take the "For Sale" sign down from the White House and the Capitol.

16. By making all of the changes above, my administration will be building a strong foundation for the American economy for the next 50 years. Changes including a more effective Congress, a simplified tax code, a rebuilt middle class, action to harness climate change, and a lower-cost health care system, just to name a few, will help build the American economy of the future—not tax cuts.

We have work to do. Change in the world continues to accelerate, and at the same time, the world is becoming smaller. The bad news is that we have serious problems in our country today. The good news is that all of these problems can be overcome with simple solutions. We need to get all of these issues on the table and move quickly to get our house in order. I have a plan, and I have the leadership skills to make the dream a reality.

If I am elected, I will work for you. I will keep you informed as to the progress of your government like no president ever has. I believe that communication is key to our success, and I will hold a monthly press conference on the first Tuesday evening of every month to update you on our progress and to answer your questions. I will put everything that I have into the job to deliver results for the American people. ✔

1

Demand a High-Performance Government

"Great vision without
great people is irrelevant."

—Jim Collins, *Good to Great: Why Some Companies
Make the Leap ... and Others Don't*[1]

The U.S. government—of the people, by the people, and for the people—should be a high-performance government. "We, the people" own our government. As a nation, we have a high-performance military, yet we tolerate poor performance in so many other areas of our government. The key to the success of any organization is the team on the field. All great organizations have a great team, and the citizens of the United States should expect nothing less from their government.

If I am elected president, I will place a high priority on making sure we have a government that operates efficiently and works for the people. Good government can make a massive difference in people's lives.

A prime example is the COVID-19 pandemic: Consider the way South Korea handled the outbreak versus the United States's response. Both countries reported their first confirmed case on January 20, 2020. South Korea's government immediately mobilized with pharmaceutical companies to develop a test; the United States government tried to build its own test, but it was flawed.

By mid-March, South Korea had tested more than 290,000 of its 50 million residents; in the U.S., 60,000 of the country's 330 million people had been tested.[2]

Within weeks, a wide gap emerged in the death rates of the two countries. As of March 31, South Korea reported 162 COVID-19 deaths[3] while U.S. fatalities from the virus topped 3,400. Top U.S. health officials said the total death count here could reach 100,000 to 240,000.[4]

As for their economies, South Korea's remained open and operating, for the most part,[5] while the U.S. business world has reeled under public lockdown orders. Government aid to U.S. companies and citizens exceeded $2 trillion as of late March, and some economists predicted more may be needed.[6]

There is a price to pay for poor government, and we are paying that price.

In my opinion, we have four major issues that lead to poor performance by our government:

1. We fail to address the big issues in our country until they become a crisis. Our government does little to prepare for the major problems that confront us.

I am reminded of the story of the manager who sits in the office all day and makes decisions. Small, easy decisions are mice, and large, complex decisions are Big Hairy Monsters. One by one, an aide brings the manager decisions to make. The aide walks in with a mouse and the manager gets his gun and shoots the mouse. Problem solved. The aide walks in with another mouse. The confident manager takes his gun out and shoots the second mouse: Another problem solved. Then the aide walks over to the closet, takes his key out and opens the door. Out pops a Big Hairy Monster of a problem. The aide leads the Big Hairy Monster to the boss. The boss looks at the Big Hairy Monster of a problem and says, "Put it back; we will deal with it another day."

This is what our government does in the United States. We fail to deal with the biggest problems of the day. Once in a while, they burst out of the closet and they scare our leaders so much that they are quickly stuffed back in the closet and nothing happens. And then one day, we get crushed. Crushed as with COVID-19; crushed like the current obesity epidemic in the United States. And we are setting ourselves up for the biggest one of them all: climate change. We know about all of these problems, but our leaders keep them in the closet because they are more interested in getting reelected than they are in doing their jobs.

Columnist Robert J. Samuelson wrote a great editorial in *The Washington Post* in September 2018 that said:

> As a society, we have failed to confront some of the major social, political and economic realities of our time: immigration, globalization, health spending, global warming, federal budget deficits, stubborn poverty and the aging of society, among others. What almost all of these issues have in common is that

the remedies they suggest are unpleasant. They demand, in the political vernacular, 'sacrifice.' To close federal budget deficits, taxes must go up and spending must come down. To deal with an aging society, people must work longer.... To resist global warming, fossil-fuel prices must go up—a lot—either through taxes or regulations.... There is no gentle way to do this.[7]

2. It is almost impossible to remove poor performers. We have a lot of great federal government employees who have put in many long hours of public service to help make America become what it is today. Unfortunately, along with the "A" and "B" players, we have too many poor performers on the team. In many government jobs—such as at the Environmental Protection Agency, the Small Business Administration, the Department of Housing and Urban Development, and the Office of Management and Budget, as well as a dozen other federal agencies—your chances of dying on the job are higher than those of being fired, according to a *USA Today* article:

The federal government fired 0.55 percent of its workers in the budget year that ended September 30, 2011. That amounted to 1,668 out of a workforce of 2.1 million. The private sector fires about 3 percent of workers annually for poor performance. That means your chance of being fired in the private sector is six times higher than your chance of being fired if you work for the federal government. The 1,800-employee Federal Communications Commission and the 1,200-employee Federal Trade Commission didn't fire a single employee. Last year, the federal government fired none of its 3,000 meteorologists, 2,500 health insurance administrators, 1,000 optometrists, 800 historians, or 500 industrial property managers.[8]

Senator John McCain (R-AZ) once said, "The failings in our civil service are encouraged by a system that makes it very difficult to fire someone even for gross misconduct. We must do away with the current system that treats federal employment as a right and makes dismissal a near impossibility."[9]

The American people own the government. The government's employees are supposed to work for us. At most high-performance companies, if you do not do your job, you get a warning. If you continue to fail to do your job, you are fired. Without the ability to fire people, the company has no leverage with the underachievers. Over time, the problem spreads, a culture of mediocrity sets in and many of the best employees leave. There is nothing that demoralizes "A" players more than having to work with slackers. So, when you can't get rid of workers who are not proficient, they stay, and the best employees leave. Since it is extremely difficult to fire government employees, there is little incentive to do an excellent job, and therefore, you are left with the potential for a poorly-performing organization. This is exactly what we have throughout our federal government today. And *you* are the owner of the team!

3. Public employee unions do not operate in the best interests of the citizens, but in their own best interests. Public employee unions make decisions and promote policies in their own best interests. They should because that is their reason for being. They bargain for the best pay, benefits, pensions, and work conditions. Unfortunately, they have used their position of influence to stack the deck against the American people. President Franklin D. Roosevelt— one of the greatest presidents this nation has ever had, who brought the country through the Great Depression and World War II, and who was a great friend of the American worker—felt that public employee unions were a bad idea. "Meticulous attention," Roosevelt said in 1937, "should be paid to the special relations and obligations of public servants to the public itself and to the government.... The process of collective bargaining, as usually understood, cannot be transplanted into the public service."[10]

4. Public employee unions use the political process to rig the game. Under the current rules, the American people cannot win with public employee unions. Public unions have significant advantages over traditional unions. Through their political activity, unions help elect the very politicians who act as management in their contract negotiations. Such power led Victor Gotbaum, the leader of District Council 37 of AFSCME (American Federation of State, County, and Municipal Employees) in New York City, to brag in 1975: "We have the ability, in a sense, to elect our own boss."[11]

Between 1990 and 2010, "public school employee unions have been the single biggest political contributors at the federal level over the past 20 years. The $56 million they've spent is roughly equal to the combined contributions of Chevron, Exxon Mobil, the National Rifle Association (NRA), and Lockheed Martin,"[12] according to an article in *The American Spectator*. The National Education Association and the American Federation of Teachers generally top the list of public employee union campaign donors, with their combined funding growing from $4.3 million in 2004 to $32 million in 2016, figures from OpenSecrets.org show.[13]

We cannot have a system in which public employee unions spend millions of dollars to influence elections to decide who their management will be and then ask that management to run a world-class organization in the best interests of the American people. For example, what if a teachers' union makes large campaign contributions to a member of Congress who sits on a committee that oversees federal education policy? Is the senator or representative going to make decisions that are in the best interest of students and their families or in the best interest of the union, helping to keep that member of Congress in office?

Steve Jobs, regarded as one of the smartest people in the last 100 years, built one of the most valuable companies in the world and reinvented five businesses in his lifetime, and he thought public teachers' unions were terrible:

> But it pains me because we do know how to provide a great education. We really do. We could make sure that every young child in this country got a great education. We fall far short of that.... The problem there, of course, is the unions. The unions are the worst thing that ever happened to education because it's not a meritocracy. It turns into a bureaucracy, which is exactly what has happened. The teachers can't teach, and administrators run the place, and nobody can be fired. It's terrible.[14]

Elsewhere, Jobs said:

> What kind of person could you get to run a small business if you told them that when they came in, they couldn't get rid of people that they thought weren't any good? Not really great ones, because if you're really smart, you go, "I can't win." What is wrong with our schools in this nation is that they have become unionized in the worst possible way.... This unionization and lifetime employment of K–12 teachers is off-the-charts crazy.[15]

Businesses need to compete in the marketplace. If someone offers a better product or a better price, the market forces you to react or go out of business. What government unions do is take competitiveness out of the game. Poorly performing areas of our government can survive because the public employee unions protect poor performers.

Because poor performers can be protected, progress is difficult to achieve, creating a less-than-awesome work environment. The government unions win, and the people lose.

If I am elected president, I will introduce the *John McCain High-Performance Government Act of 2021* within my first week on the job. The following five initiatives will create more change in the way our government operates than in the last 100 years and will produce a high-performance government that our citizens deserve:

1. Adopt the management practice of objectives and key results for every area of the federal government. John Doerr, a leading venture capitalist in Silicon Valley, wrote a book called *Measure What Matters*.[16] In the book, Doerr describes his simple management method of objectives and key results. An objective is simply what is to be achieved—no more and no less. A key result is how we get to the objective. Key results are specific, have a due date, and are measurable. Successful companies and organizations like Intel, Google, and the Gates Foundation have used this method.[17] I have successfully implemented this program at Trek, and it has made a big difference.

If I am elected president, I will make sure that those who report to me directly have objectives for the areas for which they are responsible and that they have key results to support each objective. I will make sure that this management method cascades its way through the entire federal government. This style of management works. When Google started, it was the eighteenth search company to begin.[18] Today, Google dominates search. What was the difference? Google utilized objectives and key results throughout the organization. The other companies did not.

If I am elected president, within the first 90 days, I will implement a system of objectives and key results throughout the federal government and I will share this information with the public. Implementing the program will significantly improve the performance of the federal government and will provide great information to the public as to how the government is performing.

2. Implement the Great Place to Work Program throughout the federal government. The Great Place to Work Institute sends confidential surveys to employees and asks over 50 questions to assess whether the organization is a great place to work. Based on the responses, the organization earns a score of 0–100. Many studies have concluded that happier employees are more productive, and the organization is more successful. We successfully implemented the Great Place to Work program at Trek in 2013 and it has made a massive difference—happier employees who are more productive, provide better service, and most importantly, deliver better overall results. I know that GPTW can make a massive difference in our government as well. By implementing the GPTW program, we will know how the government ranks compared to businesses; we will be able to compare one department to another; and we will be able to compare one manager to another. It is also a great way to collect employee feedback on areas to improve. If I am elected president, I will implement the Great Place to Work survey across the federal government within the first 90 days of my administration.

3. Abolish public employee unions at the federal level. We have a government of the people, by the people, and for the people. Those who work for the government are already represented by

United States Government Performance Review

OPEN TO NEW IDEAS	SCORE 0-5
Has a continuous learning engine; actively seeks new ideas	☐
Is open to ideas from anywhere	☐
Demonstrates a commitment to benchmarking other organizations' best practices	☐
Will listen to feedback and new ideas without becoming defensive	☐

PRODUCTION	SCORE 0-5
Takes initiative to go above and beyond on a consistent basis	☐
Gets things done fast, turning ideas into reality	☐
Keeps commitments and meets deadlines	☐

ENERGY	SCORE 0-5
Inspires and motivates others with positive energy	☐
Has a high sense of urgency	☐
Leaves drama at the door during conversations and interactions	☐

DECISION MAKING	SCORE 0-5
Considers multiple sources of information before making important decisions	☐
Demonstrates good judgment and common sense when making decisions	☐
Great at Plan B and adjusting when things change	☐
Deals with reality and makes the tough calls	☐

CUSTOMER SERVICE	SCORE 0-5
Has strong, productive relationships with others in organization	☐
Seeks new and innovative ways to serve customers	☐
Demonstrates the ability to make customers wildly successful	☐

OVERALL AVERAGE	SCORE

Three focus areas to improve:

1.
2.
3.

the government and should not be allowed to organize. Franklin Roosevelt was opposed to government unions at the federal level for good reasons.

4. Establish competitive wages and benefits for government workers based on the private sector and administered by the Department of Labor. We want a government that demands excellent performance and pays our workers well. Take any job and compare it to the private sector, and then set the pay and benefits at the average of what workers in the private sector make. If the current workers like the program, great; if they do not, they should look for another job—just like everyone else in the economy. Give the Department of Labor six months to come up with a simple, competitive compensation program for all federal employees.

5. Administer a simple review process for all federal employees. This process should follow these steps:

    a. Every public employee gets a simple, annual review on one page.

    b. If a manager wants to remove an employee for poor performance, the employee first gets an initial warning. The manager should specify those issues that must be addressed, and the employee would then have 60 days to improve his or her performance. Failure to meet the expectations would result in removal from the job. The manager makes the call with approval from his or her supervisor.

We live in a world where over the past 20 years, virtually every product or service has improved, become more affordable, or both. In the private sector, if your product has not improved or become more affordable, you are out of business. Good government matters to every citizen in this country. The coronavirus pandemic shows just how important it is to every American to have a competent, responsive government. If we take these steps, the citizens of this country can take back and significantly improve the government that was created to serve the people. ✓

2

Initiate Climate Change Leadership FAST!

"The greatest threat to our planet
is the belief that someone
else will save it."

—Robert Swan, the first explorer to walk
to both the North and South Poles[1]

According to NASA, 97 percent of scientists in America believe that we humans are contributing to global climate change.[2]

Thomas Friedman, in his book *Thank You for Being Late*, tells the story about London-based investor and environmentalist Adam Sweidan and the "black elephant."

Sweidan's definition of a "black elephant" is a cross between a "black swan"—a rare, low probability, unanticipated event with enormous ramifications—and "the elephant in the room: a problem that is widely visible to everyone, yet that no one wants to address, even though we absolutely know that one day it will have vast, black-swan-like consequences." Sweidan told Friedman that "there are a herd of environmental black elephants gathering out there. Global warming, deforestation, ocean acidification, and mass biodiversity extinction, just to name four. When they hit, we'll claim they were black swans that no one could have predicted, but in fact they are black elephants, very visible right now."[3]

It is my opinion that the vast majority of our political leaders have failed us by not informing the public of the massive negative consequences that will occur if we continue along our current path of inaction when it comes to global climate change. No one in the United States government is providing the leadership that is equal to the severity of the climate change challenge. The ramifications for every person in our country and on our planet are significant if the current course of inaction continues.

What are the facts to back up Sweidan's claim that we are facing a "black elephant" and that climate change is one of the greatest issues of our time, and why we should act now and do something about this?

1. Researchers at the Mauna Loa Observatory in Hawaii have measured carbon dioxide levels in the atmosphere since 1958. The first measurements showed the amount of carbon dioxide in the atmosphere at 315 parts per million. In 2006, the level was 380, and in May 2019, the level hit a record 414.7 parts per million, up from 411.2 in May 2018.[4]

Scientists believe we are already in the red zone. If nothing is done, and the level of carbon continues to rise, the temperature on the planet will rise significantly in the next 50 years, and the impact will be catastrophic. An increase from 315 to 414.7 parts per million over the past 60 years doesn't seem like a lot. But when you look at the graph on page 48, it is eye-opening.

Percentage of climate scientists who agree that climate-warming trends over the past century are **likely due to human activities.**

What really scares me is not the 60-year graph but the graph looking at carbon levels in the atmosphere over the last 2,000 years, which shows that the level of carbon was around 250 for most of the last 2,000 years and then started to significantly move up over the last 60 years. If you asked a mathematician to study this data and estimate where the amount of carbon will be in 50 years, the answer would be over 500 parts per million. The effect of that much carbon in the atmosphere will be catastrophic to human life on Earth.

2. The temperature of our planet has increased by 2 degrees since 1880.[5] Eight of the last 10 years have been the hottest the world has experienced in 140 years of record keeping, the National Oceanic and Atmospheric Administration (NOAA) said in January, with 2019 coming in second only to 2016's record high heat.[6] While 2 degrees over 140 years may not sound like a lot, consider that the optimal temperature for the human body is 98.6 degrees. If you increased that to 100.6, you would be sick. That is where we are as a planet today. We have a temperature of 100.6, and we are sick. What is worse is that the doctors (global scientists) are telling us that if we don't change some of our habits, our temperature will be 105.2 by the year 2100. The human body dies at 108. What happens when Earth's temperature rises? Heat waves, forest fires, changes in the patterns of rainfall and snowfall, more intense storms, a more hospitable environment for transmitting infectious diseases such as COVID-19,[7] and the extinction of various plants and animals. In fact, since 1970, there has been a 60 percent loss in mammal, fish, reptile, bird and amphibian population.[8]

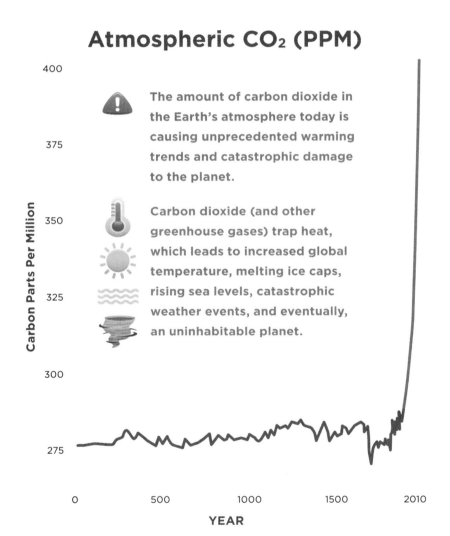

Atmospheric CO_2 (PPM)

The amount of carbon dioxide in the Earth's atmosphere today is causing unprecedented warming trends and catastrophic damage to the planet.

Carbon dioxide (and other greenhouse gases) trap heat, which leads to increased global temperature, melting ice caps, rising sea levels, catastrophic weather events, and eventually, an uninhabitable planet.

Carbon Parts Per Million

YEAR

Source: Kennedy, R (Director). (2018). *Above and Beyond: NASA's Journey to Tomorrow* [Motion Picture]. United States: Fathom Events

CO₂ Emissions per Capita

Average carbon dioxide (CO₂)emissions per capita
measured in tonnes per year.

1 metric tonne = 1,000 kilograms or 2204.6 pounds

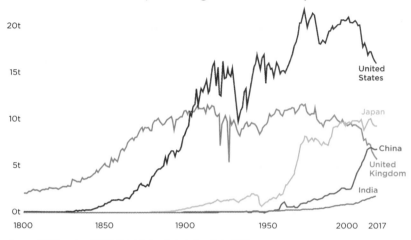

Source: OWID based on CDIAC; Global Carbon Project; Gapminder & UN

3. The effects of climate change are happening today across our country. Our communities are feeling the effects of climate change now. Since 1900, the global sea level has risen 8 inches, with nearly half of that increase coming since 1993.[9] Coastal cities across America are feeling the effects of flooding and the increased intensity of hurricanes. Houston, Texas, is a great example. That area has suffered three 500-year floods from 2015 to 2017.[10] Midwestern farmers have felt the effects of crop-damaging heat waves, and wildfires have ravaged communities in the West. In 2017, California experienced the worst wildfires in its history—9,000 fires, nearly 1.4 million acres burned, over 10,000 structures destroyed, and 47 people dead.[11] Then, 2018 was even worse for California, with nearly 1.9 million acres burned, more than 22,000 buildings destroyed, and 103 lives lost.[12] Fifteen of the biggest fires in California history have occurred in the past 18 years.[13]

The average U.S. temperature for 2017 was 54.6 degrees, 2.6 degrees above the 20th-century average. In 2017, five states had their warmest year on record, and 16 weather and climate disasters cost more than $306 billion, which broke the record set in 2005 of $215 billion.[14]

4. The United States is the second-largest polluter in the world, emitting 5,319 million metric tons of carbon dioxide into the atmosphere in 2018.[15] The average American citizen emits 15.7 metric tons of carbon per year compared to the average German, who emits 9.7 metric tons; the average Japanese, who releases 10.4 metric tons; and the average person in the U.K., who is responsible for 5.7 metric tons, based on global 2017 statistics.[16]

5. Climate change is costing us a fortune and is sucking up massive resources. Over the past decade, extreme weather and the health impact of burning fossil fuels have cost the American economy at least $240 billion per year. It is estimated that over the next decade, the cost will increase by at least 50 percent.[17]

6. Scientists are telling us that the environment will face greater pressure in the future. It is projected that the world's total population will increase from 7.7 billion today to 9.7 billion by 2050.[18] In 30 years, we will have an additional 2 billion people living on Earth. As Friedman writes in *Thank You for Being Late*, "The impact on the planet's natural systems and climate will become exponentially more devastating, because more and more of those 9.7 billion are moving to large urban areas and up the socioeconomic ladder where they will drive more cars, live in more and bigger homes, consume more water and electricity, and eat more protein. Today, roughly 86 percent of Americans have air-conditioning in their homes and apartments, compared to only 7 percent in Brazil and less than that in India."[19] What happens when the rest of the world starts to consume like Americans?

7. The trend is not our friend. Our global leaders are failing us. In 2017, carbon emissions increased by 1.4 percent globally. This might not sound like a big deal, but it is the equivalent of adding 170 million cars on the road.[20]

Levels of CO_2 kicked up another 2.1 percent in 2018 and 0.6 percent in 2019, according to the Global Carbon Budget 2019.[21] This also

A Lifetime of Plastic

The first plastics made from fossil fuels are just over a century old. They came into widespread use after World War II and are found today in everything from cars to medical devices to food packaging. Their useful lifetime varies. Once disposed of, they break down into smaller fragments that linger for centuries.

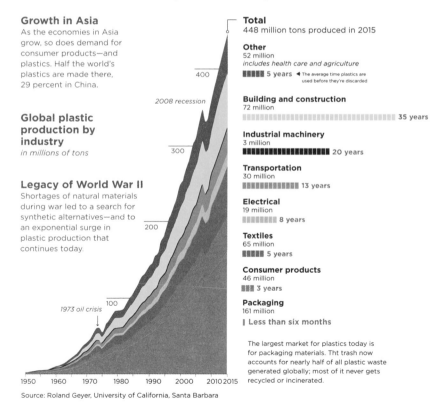

Growth in Asia
As the economies in Asia grow, so does demand for consumer products—and plastics. Half the world's plastics are made there, 29 percent in China.

Global plastic production by industry
in millions of tons

Legacy of World War II
Shortages of natural materials during war led to a search for synthetic alternatives—and to an exponential surge in plastic production that continues today.

2008 recession

1973 oil crisis

Total
448 million tons produced in 2015

Other
52 million
includes health care and agriculture
▮▮▮▮▮ 5 years ◀ The average time plastics are used before they're discarded

Building and construction
72 million
▮▮▮▮▮▮▮▮▮▮▮▮▮▮▮▮▮▮▮▮▮▮▮▮▮▮▮▮▮▮▮▮▮▮▮ 35 years

Industrial machinery
3 million
▮▮▮▮▮▮▮▮▮▮▮▮▮▮▮▮▮▮▮▮ 20 years

Transportation
30 million
▮▮▮▮▮▮▮▮▮▮▮▮▮ 13 years

Electrical
19 million
▮▮▮▮▮▮▮▮ 8 years

Textiles
65 million
▮▮▮▮▮ 5 years

Consumer products
46 million
▮▮▮ 3 years

Packaging
161 million
▮ Less than six months

The largest market for plastics today is for packaging materials. Tht trash now accounts for nearly half of all plastic waste generated globally; most of it never gets recycled or incinerated.

Source: Roland Geyer, University of California, Santa Barbara

comes on the heels of the U.S. leaving the Paris Agreement, a 2016 agreement that nearly 200 countries signed, pledging to combat climate change.[22] As a global community and as a country, we are going the wrong way, and we do not have a sense of urgency. Leadership is the ability to make the dream a reality at the grassroots level. The facts say that we have a massive global crisis on our hands, but the reality at the grassroots level is that not much has changed. Translation: Failed global leadership and failed leadership in the United States.

8. Foreign policy and military implications. Top military officials have warned for years that climate change will have serious ramifications for the United States military.[23] Climate change leads

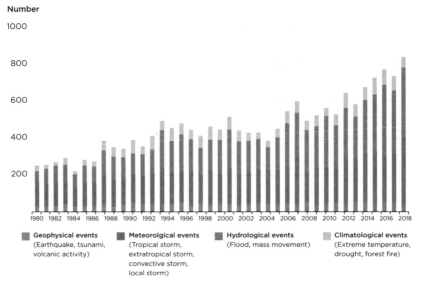

Number of World Natural Catastrophes, 1980-2018

Numbers of events that have caused at least one death and/or major dollar loss

Source: © 2019 Munich Re, Geo Risks Research, NatCatSERVICE. As of March 2019.

to extreme weather events, which lead to humanitarian disasters and state failures, which increase the likelihood of extremism and terrorism. Here's one example: Between 2006 and 2009, Syria suffered a terrible drought that scientists blame on human-induced climate change. The drought, combined with government policies that hurt farmers, forced more than 1 million rural Syrians to flee to cities, multiplying the stresses that sparked the 2011 uprising against the Syrian government. The continuing civil war has claimed the lives of more than 500,000 Syrians, a watchdog group says, and has displaced more than 12 million, United Nations figures show.[24] When the U.S. military describes climate change as a "threat multiplier," Syria is the perfect example of more humanitarian disasters and stress on the U.S. military as global climate change speeds up. Add onto the pile that a large percentage of the carbon we burn comes from unstable regimes around the world. Reducing our carbon emissions would mean that we would lessen our dependence on foreign oil and would increase global stability.

9. There is a moral reason to address climate change now. The United States is the second-largest polluter in the world behind China, and we are close to the top of the list when you look at carbon emissions per person. The carbon that we spew into the atmosphere does not just pollute our air, it affects every global citizen. As a country, we have a moral responsibility to clean up the mess that we have created.

Our generation will either be known as the generation that looked at the facts, acted with a sense of urgency and turned the environmental tide, or we will be known as the generation that stood still, ignored the facts, and failed to lead at one of the most defining moments in world history. António Guterres, the Secretary-General of the United Nations, said, "We are still not doing enough, nor moving fast enough, to prevent irreversible and catastrophic climate disruption."[25]

If I am elected president, I will make the environment a top priority. We need to shift away from our dependence on fossil fuels that create greenhouse gases and replace fossil fuels with clean energy from the sun, the wind, and the water. These are the action items on climate change that you can expect from me if I am elected president:

1. I will make climate change a top priority of my administration. My administration will work hard within the United States to prioritize a response to climate change. We will also work with other nations to address the crisis. Climate change is not just a United States issue, or a Chinese issue, or a German issue; it is a global issue. Air does not have boundaries. Hurricanes do not pick countries. The climate is changing because, as global citizens, we are pouring more carbon dioxide into the atmosphere than the planet can handle. We need every country involved in the solution, and I will make sure the United States is at the table taking a leadership role. The UN's Guterres said, "What is missing—still, even after the clinching of the Paris Agreement—is leadership, a sense of urgency and a true commitment to a decisive multilateral response."[26] My administration will provide leadership and a sense of urgency to make global climate change one of our top priorities. If we do not solve global climate change, the ramifications on our planet, our country, and our families will be devastating.

2. Re-sign the Paris Agreement. Within the first 30 days of my administration, we will rejoin the rest of the global community and re-sign the Paris Agreement. If I am elected president, the United States will no longer take the position that climate change is a hoax. Our planet is sick, and its sickness is not isolated to certain countries or parts of the globe. It affects every country and every citizen. Because we have the largest economy in the world, because we are the second-largest polluter in the world, because we are citizens of the world, and because we have always led the world in great endeavors, my administration will put America back into the Paris Agreement and will be out in front asking other nations to join the effort.

3. My administration, in its first 90 days, will ask Congress to implement the *Baker-Shultz Carbon Dividend Plan.* Former Secretary of State James Baker and former Secretary of State George Shultz have joined with former Treasury Secretary Hank Paulson, former Walmart chairman Rob Walton, former Vice President Al Gore, leading environmental groups, and a few large oil companies, including ExxonMobil, BP, and Royal Dutch Shell, to support a simple carbon tax of $40 per ton. The plan has three basic parts:[27]

a. The federal government would impose a tax on carbon dioxide emissions, beginning at $40 per ton on July 1, 2021. I would propose to increase it to $60 per ton on July 1, 2023, $80 per ton on July 1, 2025, and $100 per ton on July 1, 2027. The tax would be collected where the fossil fuels enter the economy, such as the mine, well, or port, and would increase prices of products containing carbon. The tax would send a clear message to both businesses and consumers that we must reduce our carbon footprint.

b. The proceeds of this tax would be significant, in the $300 billion range per year, and would be returned to the American people via a quarterly dividend. It is estimated that a family of four would receive $2,000 in the first year to offset the higher costs of products that contain carbon. Those families reducing their carbon footprint would benefit the most.

c. American companies exporting to countries without comparable carbon programs would receive rebates to make sure that American companies are competing on a level playing field. This would also send a strong message to other nations to adopt the same carbon tax as the United States.

There are a few reasons why I believe that the *Baker-Shultz Carbon Dividend Plan* is the right plan to address the climate change issue. First, it is nonpartisan. Smart people from both sides of the aisle support this idea as well as oil companies and large retailers like Walmart. Second, it is simple. One simple tax can significantly reduce the amount of carbon dioxide that we put into the atmosphere. Instead of coming up with hundreds of government programs, we can come up with one straightforward tax.

4. Endorse the *One Trillion Tree program.* My administration will endorse and promote the simple concept of planting one trillion trees during this decade. As Al Gore has said, "The best available technology for pulling carbon dioxide from the air is something called a tree."[28] Planting trees is simple, effective, and most importantly, it is economical and something that everyone can do.

Today, global climate change is the greatest long-term threat we face. It's affecting us every day, and if nothing is done, it will continue to get worse. For too long, our leaders have failed to sound the alarm that this topic needs our attention now. The world has sounded the alarm on the coronavirus, and world leaders are moving quickly to contain the pandemic. Climate change has implications 1,000 times as serious as the coronavirus, yet we cannot get the car out of the garage to address climate change. Why not? Because as a nation, we only address short-term crises that make the news and we fail to address the BIG, long-term threats that have massive implications on our future As a nation, we were the determining factor in winning

World War I and World War II. As a nation, we won the race to put a man on the moon, we preserved the peace, and ended the Cold War. We have done more than any other country to promote peace throughout the world and to raise hundreds of millions of people out of poverty. It is time that we once again rally the global community to turn the tide against global climate change. It can be done! ✔

3

Reduce the Risk
of Nuclear War

"It's a near miracle that nuclear
war has so far been avoided."

—Noam Chomsky, linguist and political theorist[1]

We have a lot of major problems in the United States: gridlock in Congress, a seemingly insurmountable budget deficit, an out-of-control legal system, and an astronomically expensive health care system—all of which can be solved if we put our minds to it. But there is one problem we have that could destroy humanity in a matter of minutes, and that is the possibility of nuclear war. The threat is so daunting that no one wants to talk about it.

Most Americans don't know these weapons exist in the numbers that they do. Most Americans thought the threat of nuclear war ended with the Cold War. The reality is that the threat of nuclear war is greater today than at any time since the Cuban Missile Crisis. More countries have nuclear weapons than in 1962, and the information on how to build a bomb is more available. The Cold War—which, ironically, contained the threat of nuclear war—is now gone. In addition, the sophistication of terrorist groups has changed the nuclear game. Many people have no idea that a single strategic nuclear warhead today is 1,000 times more powerful than the bomb dropped on Hiroshima, Japan, ending World War II.[2] We no longer talk about the massive nuclear arsenals that exist in the world. For some reason, we are focused on issues that make for sensational short-term news: mass shootings, natural disasters, and plane crashes, to name a few. As a society, we think too short-term and focus on headline news instead of on the most important issues. Nuclear weapons and the potential that someone could blow up the world should be near the top of any president's list.

On January 23, 2020, the "Bulletin of the Atomic Scientists"—whose Board of Sponsors includes 13 Nobel Prize recipients—moved the Doomsday Clock from two minutes to midnight to 100 seconds before midnight. This announcement marks the most severe security threat in the Doomsday Clock's history, greater than during the Cuban Missile Crisis, or at any time in the Cold War. The statement from the "Bulletin of the Atomic Scientists" said, "Humanity continues to face two simultaneous existential dangers—nuclear war and climate change—that are compounded by a threat multiplier, cyber-enabled information warfare, that undercuts society's ability to respond. The international security situation is dire, not just because these threats exist, but because world leaders have allowed the international political infrastructure for managing them to erode."[3]

The report cites unrest on the Korean Peninsula, the deteriorating relationship between the United States and Russia, tensions between the United States and China in the South China Sea, Pakistan and India adding to their arsenals, and the end of the U.S.-Iran nuclear agreement. Every American should be concerned about the

Doomsday Clock and what the United States government is doing—or is not doing—to reduce the chances of nuclear war.

> Einstein was once asked how World War III would be fought. His answer: "I do not know how the Third World War will be fought, but I can tell you what they will use in the Fourth—rocks."[4]

As president, I will prioritize the elimination of the chance of a nuclear war in our lifetime. Below are the reasons why we should all be concerned about the threat of nuclear war:

1. Accidents happen. In 1961, a U.S. Air Force B-52 airplane broke up in midair over Goldsboro, North Carolina. It was carrying two Mark 39 hydrogen bombs, and each would have been 260 times more powerful than the Hiroshima bomb. Thankfully, they did not detonate.[5] During the Cold War, eight nuclear weapons were lost. During the attempted assassination of President Reagan in March 1981, the laminated card, which contains authentication codes to identify the president in case of a nuclear order, was taken from him; it was later found in a plastic hospital bag.[6] In 1979, President Carter's national security adviser Zbigniew Brzezinski was awakened by a phone call in the middle of the night warning of an all-out Soviet nuclear attack. He received a second call confirming the attack and informing him of the imminent nuclear destruction of the United States. Shortly before calling the president, Brzezinski received a

In 1961 a U.S. Air Force B-52 broke up in midair over Goldsboro, North Carolina. It was carrying two Mark 39 hydrogen bombs, and each would have been **260 times more powerful than Hiroshima.**

third call canceling the alarm. It was a mistake caused by human and technical error.[7] We can recover from almost all accidents. Unfortunately, we might not be able to recover from a nuclear accident. It could be the end of the world as we know it.

2. Weapons that are developed end up being used. Hiram Maxim, who invented the machine gun, said, "Only a general who was a barbarian would send his men to certain death against the concentrated power of my new gun."[8] Orville Wright had thoughts similar to Maxim's: "When my brother and I built and flew the first man-carrying flying machine, we thought we were introducing in the world an invention that would make further wars practically impossible."[9] Just as with the machine gun, the airplane did not end war; it made war kill even more people. On March 9, 1945, more than 90,000 people were killed, and 25 percent of Tokyo was destroyed by bombs dropped from the same planes that Orville Wright thought might make war impractical.[10] Today, there are nearly 4,000 nuclear warheads deployed, on missiles or at military bases around the world, and another 10,000 in storage or waiting to be dismantled.[11] We are betting that they will not be used. History would say that we are crazy.

3. The amount of time in which a decision can be made regarding the use of nuclear weapons is limited. It is estimated that the president would have 12 minutes to make a decision to launch U.S. nuclear missiles.[12] A Minuteman III nuclear weapon travels at a speed of 15,000 miles per hour, and the Trident II missile is believed to top that, with speeds as high as 18,000 miles per hour.[13] If you think that a nuclear crisis will never happen, all you need to do is look back at the Cuban Missile Crisis. We were so close to a nuclear war that President Kennedy estimated the odds of nuclear war as being "somewhere between one out of three and even."[14]

A Trident II nuclear weapon travels at a speed of 18,000 miles per hour

4. It is not just the United States and Russia that have the bomb. Who else has nuclear weapons? China, the U.K., France, India, Pakistan, North Korea, and Israel.[15] With the increasing level of global terrorism, we have to worry not only about the 3,750 nuclear weapons on active duty worldwide,[16] but we need to worry about every nuclear weapon in the world, and that is becoming more difficult to do.

5. Computer systems have problems, and when you are talking about nuclear war, a systems problem could be the end of the world. A computer system failure could trigger a nuclear war. According to Martin Hellman, an expert on issues surrounding nuclear war, "In 1979 and the first half of 1980, there were 3,703 low-level false alerts in the United States alone."[17] Hellman also has written, "In 1995, Russian air defense mistook a meteorological rocket launched from Norway for a U.S. submarine-launched ballistic missile. Russian President Boris Yeltsin was notified, and a device containing the codes for authorizing a nuclear attack was opened. Fortunately, Yeltsin made the right call, and nothing happened."[18]

6. The U.S. nuclear weapons program costs a fortune. According to the Congressional Budget Office (CBO), the United States military budgeted $33.6 billion on the nuclear force in 2019. The Congressional Budget Office's projected cost of the U.S. nuclear force for the next 10 years is $494 billion. The CBO estimates the cost of modernizing the U.S. nuclear arsenal could reach $1.2 trillion over the next 30 years.[19]

$494 billion

The Congressional budget's projected cost of the U.S. nuclear force for the next 10 years.

7. The greatest nuclear threat today is not the Russians, but the terrorists. In February 2006, Oleg Khinsagov, a Russian national, was arrested for possession of 79.5 grams of weapons-grade uranium. Khinsagov's intent was to sell the material for $1 million.[20] This is a real story, and this stuff can happen. There is nuclear material all over the world, and the threat of a person who works in a nuclear lab with access to this material selling it to a bad guy is greater than zero. We live in a different world today, and the number one threat of a nuclear explosion is not from the Russians, but from the same extremists who cut the heads off of innocent people; from ISIS, who killed 129 people in the Paris attacks on November 13, 2015;[21] and from Al-Qaeda, which killed 2,996 people on September 11, 2001.[22]

8. We could use the $40 billion a year, on average, that nuclear weapons will cost us for more important projects. Colin Powell, who served as Secretary of State and as chairman of the Joint Chiefs of Staff, had 28,000 nuclear weapons under his command. After leaving office and upon further reflection, General Powell said, "The one thing I convinced myself after all these years of exposure to the use of nuclear weapons is that they are useless."[23] We are currently working on a plan to spend more than $1 trillion over the next 30 years to modernize our nuclear forces. Imagine what we as a country could do with $40 billion every year for the next 10 years.

The United States is the most powerful nation in the world. We have used that power over the last century to bring an end to World Wars I and II. We have used that power to bring communism to its knees and end the Cold War. Part of our nation's fabric is that we are leaders. If I am elected president, I will use the power of the presidency to significantly reduce the threat of nuclear war. In the 2010 documentary *Nuclear Tipping Point*, Henry Kissinger says:

> "Once nuclear weapons are used, we will be driven to take global measures to prevent it. So some of us have said … 'If we have to do it afterwards, why don't we do it now?'"[24]

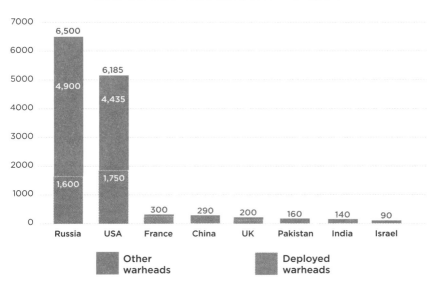

Stockpile of Destruction

Estimated Global Nuclear Warheads
2019 Defense News story on SIPRI report

Source: SIPRI. https://www.defensenews.com/global/2019/06/16/heres-how-many-nuclear-warheads-exist-and-which-countries-own-them/

As president, I will focus on these three simple steps to dramatically reduce the threat of nuclear war and set a good example for the rest of the world:

1. On my first day as president, I will reduce the U.S. nuclear arsenal from 6,185 to around 300 immediately. Gary Schaub Jr. and James Forsyth Jr., civilian employees of the U.S. Air Force, wrote an op-ed in *The New York Times* on May 23, 2010, in which they recommended reducing to around 300 the number of nuclear weapons to be deployed on land, sea, and airplanes.[25] By decreasing our nuclear fleet in this way, we will decrease the chances of a nuclear accident initiated by the United States by 95 percent.

2. I will sign U.N. Resolution 62/36, agreeing that the United States will not use nuclear weapons as a first-strike option and will only use them if someone detonates a nuclear warhead on U.S. land. This agreement would end the possibility of nuclear war being waged over a misguided perceived threat or a misunderstood provocation. In 2008, 139 countries voted for U.N. Resolution 62/36, which would remove nuclear weapons from "high-alert, quick-launch status." Only three nations voted against the measure: the U.S., the U.K., and France.[26] I will take quick and decisive action to join the 139 other nations and reduce the threat of nuclear war by signing U.N. Resolution 62/36.

3. I will set the goal of creating a nuclear weapons-free world by 2024, and my administration will take a leadership role in making it happen. We have done so many awesome things in our 243 years as a nation. Why not lead the world in creating a nuclear weapons-free world? We will lead by example by reducing our nuclear arsenal on day one of my administration as well as signing

U.N. Resolution 62/36. When the world sees that the United States has reduced its nuclear force by 95 percent and that the United States has agreed not to use a first-strike option, we will gain credibility to lead this effort. A Harvard University study in 2010 estimated that at that point, the cost of securing all nuclear weapons and nuclear materials over a four-year period would be about $10 billion.[27]

I will propose to the leaders of the G20 that we set a global goal of eliminating nuclear weapons by 2024 and that we create the Global Nuclear-Free Fund and buy up all the nuclear weapons in the world. If our nuclear arsenal already costs more than $30 billion a year to maintain, I believe that as a nation, we would be better off spending $10 billion to rid the world of nuclear weapons than we would be spending an estimated $494 billion over the next 10 years to modernize weapons that we never plan to use.

In 1961, in a speech to the United Nations, President Kennedy warned of the devastation that would result from a nuclear war:

> Today, every inhabitant of this planet must contemplate the day when this planet may no longer be habitable. Every man, woman, and child lives under a nuclear sword of Damocles, hanging by the slenderest of threads, capable of being cut at any moment by accident or miscalculation or by madness. The weapons of war must be abolished before they abolish us.
>
> Men no longer debate whether armaments are a symptom or a cause of tension. The mere existence of modern weapons— 10 million times more powerful than any that the world has ever seen, and only minutes away from any target on earth—is a source of horror, and discord, and distrust. Men no longer maintain that disarmament must await the settlement of all disputes—for disarmament must be a part of any permanent settlement. And

men may no longer pretend that the quest for disarmament is a sign of weakness—for in a spiraling arms race, a nation's security may well be shrinking even as its arms increase.

For 15 years this organization (The United Nations) has sought the reduction and destruction of arms. Now that goal is no longer a dream—it is a practical matter of life or death. The risks inherent in disarmament pale in comparison to the risks inherent in an unlimited arms race.[28]

Nearly 60 years have passed since President Kennedy spoke of the threat of nuclear war. Unfortunately, we are no closer to abolishing nuclear weapons before they abolish us. The cold, hard reality is that we are further away. While there may be fewer bombs today, they are more powerful now than at any other time in history. More nations have the bomb, and the potential for new nations and terrorist groups to get the bomb is higher today than at any other point in history. We continue to play a game of nuclear roulette, and at some point in time, if we continue to do nothing to reduce the risk, the gun will go off.

This generation of Americans should be the generation that eliminates nuclear weapons from the face of the earth, not the generation that stands by, does nothing, and hopes we can kick the can on to the next generation. As president, I will work hard to make the dream a reality. It is the greatest gift our generation could pass on to the next. ✅

4

Fix the Health Care System

"My goal has always been to help people help themselves. Your body is your most priceless possession, you've got to take care of it."

—Jack LaLanne, physical fitness guru[1]

If I am elected president, I will bring massive change to our health care system. In America, we spend more money than any nation on our health care, and we get horrible results. We spent $11,172 per person for health care in 2018, which amounts to 17.7 percent of our GDP (gross domestic product), according to the Centers for Medicare and Medicaid Services.[2] This ranks the highest in the world, by far.[3]

Yet, for all of the money we spend, our average life expectancy is 78.6 years, below that of 28 other countries, including Germany, Japan and the United Kingdom.[4]

In fact, the United States is scraping the bottom of the barrel, tied for 54th place of the 56 countries surveyed in Bloomberg's 2018 Health-Efficiency Index, which is based on 2015 global data.[5]

Our government's failure to react swiftly to COVID-19 made the situation even worse—leaving the nation's hospitals with inadequate equipment to treat patients and insufficient protection for health care workers.[6] This is another example of the highest cost health care system in the world unable to deliver top-notch care.

Our friends in Hong Kong spend $2,222 per person and achieve a life expectancy of 84.3 years, the highest in the survey. Canada's system produces 3.5 years longer life expectancy than the U.S. and costs almost 60 percent less, the Bloomberg analysis shows. People in Greece spend only $1,505, on average, and can expect to live to age 81.[7]

	🇺🇸	🇨🇦
Life expectancy	**78.6**	**82.8**
Health care cost as a % of GDP	17.7%	11.3%
Health care cost per person	$11,172	$4,804[8]

Companies study their competitors all the time. Similarly, sports teams look at their competitors and adopt their winning strategies. They have an open mind in searching for the best solutions. It is time that we took our heads out of the sand and looked at other countries for best practices with regard to health care and put them to work in America.

Our life expectancy in the U.S. dropped for three years in a row, in 2015-2017. That's the longest consecutive yearly decline in the projected length of the average American's life since the period between 1915 and 1918, when World War I and the Spanish flu pandemic claimed millions of lives, worldwide.[9]

The news gets worse: We are raising the unhealthiest generation of Americans in our history. If we think of the U.S. health care system as an athletic team competing in a league, then we would be baseball's New York Yankees, outspending every other team, year in and year out, but unlike the Yankees, we end up near the bottom of the league every single year. The worst part about it is that year after year, we tolerate being the highest paid team with some of the worst results, and we do nothing serious about changing the equation. This would never happen in sports or in business, and yet we tolerate this poor performance in our nation's health care system.

Despite having the highest costs in the world with close to the worst results, no one is addressing the real problems of our health care system. As President Barack Obama said, "The greatest threat to

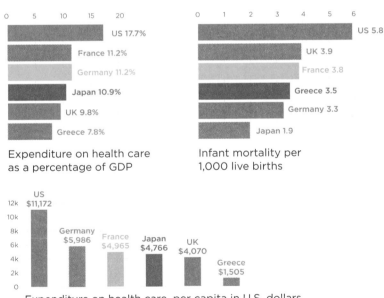

World Health

Health care comparisons around the world

Expenditure on health care as a percentage of GDP

US 17.7%
France 11.2%
Germany 11.2%
Japan 10.9%
UK 9.8%
Greece 7.8%

Infant mortality per 1,000 live births

US 5.8
UK 3.9
France 3.8
Greece 3.5
Germany 3.3
Japan 1.9

Expenditure on health care, per capita in U.S. dollars

US $11,172
Germany $5,986
France $4,965
Japan $4,766
UK $4,070
Greece $1,505

Sources: CMS (Centers for Medicare and Medicaid Services);
CMS, Organization for Economic Co-operation and Development, 2018;
OECD https://data.oecd.org/healthres/health-spending.htm;
https://data.oecd.org/healthstat/infant-mortality-rates.htm, 2017

America's fiscal health is not Social Security…. It's not the investments that we've made to rescue our economy during this crisis. By a wide margin, the biggest threat to our nation's balance sheet is the skyrocketing cost of health care. It is not even close."[10] And what have we done as a country regarding what Obama said is the biggest threat to our nation's balance sheet? Basically nothing.

Gary Player, a golf legend and health fanatic, lamented the health of Americans:

> America is maybe the most unhealthy nation in the world because they live on crap. They've got the best food in the world, the best farmers, but they live on crap. When (British chef) Jamie Oliver went to America, he went to areas where children never had cabbage or broccoli or spinach or vegetables in their lives. People are giving their children a soft drink and a doughnut to go to school. No wonder academically they're affected….

> Fifty-five percent of the greatest country in the world is obese? How can you compete against the Chinese? You haven't got a chance! People that are lean and mean and working hard and producing maybe 100 engineers to every two or three that you produce. Kids that are learning like crazy at school and spending hours learning. You go to Korea, and those kids finish school at 7 o'clock at night because there's no sense of entitlement. It frustrates me because I happen to have 15 American grandchildren. I love America, but I get so upset at the way I see the obesity. I just don't see how the health care system can work. I pray it does, but I just don't see how it can work with this tsunami of obesity.[11]

Health Care Costs by Year

National Health Care Spending			
Year	(Billions)	Percent Growth	Cost Per Person
1960	$27.2	NA	$146
1965	$41.9	9.0%	$209
1970	$74.6	13.1%	$355
1975	$133.3	14.4%	$605
1980	$255.3	15.3%	$1,108
1985	$442.9	9.4%	$1,833
1990	$721.4	11.9%	$2,843
1995	$1,021.6	5.6%	$3,806
2000	$1,369.7	7.1%	$4,857
2005	$2,024.2	6.7%	$6,855
2010	$2,598.8	4.1%	$8,412
2015	$3,200.8	5.8%	$9,994
2018	$3,650.0	4.5%	$11,172

Source: "National Health Expenditures Summary Including Share of GDP, CY 1960-2017," Centers for Medicare and Medicaid Services.19 "Inflation Rate by Year," The Balance. "History of Health Spending in the United States, 1960-2013," Centers for Medicare and Medicaid Services, November 19, 2015.20 "U.S. Health Care Spending: Who Pays?"21 California Health Care Foundation, December 2015.

Gary Player is right. The health of America is a disaster, and our health care system is failing us. How bad is the health care system in America? Here are six key reasons why if I am elected president, I will make radical changes to our current health care system:

1. Our health care costs are out of control. We spend $3.65 trillion per year on health care, more as a percentage of GDP than any other country in the Western world, and we get close to the worst results.[12] When Medicare became law in 1965, the program was predicted to cost $12 billion in 1990. This estimate proved to be not even close. The true cost of Medicare that year actually was $110 billion.[13]

In a 2015 article in *The New Yorker* magazine, Dr. Atul Gawande—a surgeon, writer, and public health researcher who is regarded as one of the smartest people in America—pointed to a study of more than one million Medicare patients that researched how often they were given any of 26 tests or treatments that "scientific and professional organizations have consistently determined to have no benefit or to be outright harmful." The study found that up to 42 percent of the patients had received unnecessary tests in one year. Gawande said his mother was one of them.[14]

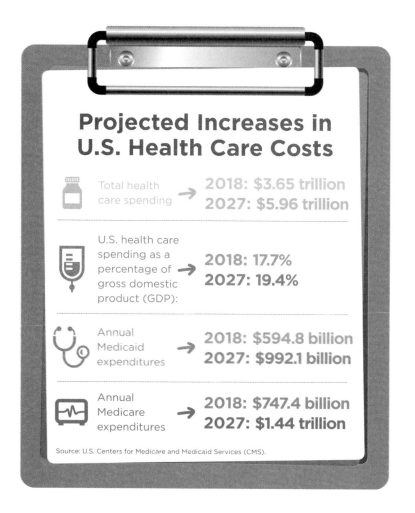

Projected Increases in U.S. Health Care Costs

Total health care spending → 2018: $3.65 trillion
2027: $5.96 trillion

U.S. health care spending as a percentage of gross domestic product (GDP): → 2018: 17.7%
2027: 19.4%

Annual Medicaid expenditures → 2018: $594.8 billion
2027: $992.1 billion

Annual Medicare expenditures → 2018: $747.4 billion
2027: $1.44 trillion

Source: U.S. Centers for Medicare and Medicaid Services (CMS).

2. The future projections for health care spending are ominous.
Health care spending has risen from five percent of our GDP in 1960 to 17.7 percent today.[15] The average annual premium for employer-sponsored health insurance in 2019, according to the Kaiser Family Foundation, was $7,188 for an individual and $20,576 for a family.[16]

The total cost in 2018 for national health expenditures, according to the U.S. government, was $3.65 trillion. The government is projecting that by 2027, the total cost for health expenditures in the United States will hit just under $6 trillion.[17] Medicare faces significant financial challenges in the coming years. Our population is getting older, and the ratio of workers to enrollees is declining. The total amount of money that our government spends on Medicare was $750.2 billion in 2018[18] and the Congressional Budget Office estimates it will increase to $1.44 trillion by 2027.[19] The CBO has written that health costs will have a huge effect on the federal budget in the coming years:

> Future growth in spending per beneficiary for Medicare and Medicaid—the federal government's major health care programs—will be the most important determinant of long-term trends in federal spending. Changing those programs in ways that reduce the growth of costs—which will be difficult, in part because of the complexity of health policy choices—is ultimately the nation's main long-term challenge in setting federal fiscal policy.

3. Americans are addicted to the health care system, drugs, and hospitals. In 2010, doctors performed more than 51 million inpatient surgical procedures in U.S. hospitals, according to the National Quality Forum, or one for every six Americans.[20] No other country in the world comes even close to operating on nearly 20 percent of its citizens per year. It is crazy. As one example, the United States conducts 71 percent more CT scans per capita than Germany does. The cost of those CT scans through Medicare is four times as much as the cost in Germany.[21]

In 2010, doctors performed at least
51 MILLION surgical
procedures

in the United States, or one for every six Americans.

If Germany has 100 patients who get a CT scan, the U.S. has 171. If the cost in Germany is $250, then in the U.S., it is $1,000, or four times as much. So a summary of the total costs looks like this:

Germany: 100 x $250 = $25,000
United States: 171 x $1,000 = $171,000

4. Our health care system is rigged by insurance companies and by politicians who receive campaign contributions from insurance companies. In 2013, journalist Steven Brill wrote an exposé of the exorbitant costs of health care in America. He reported that since 1998, the pharmaceutical and health care industries "have spent $5.36 billion … on lobbying Washington." In comparison, during the same period, the defense industry spent $1.53 billion on lobbying efforts. As Brill summed up: "That's right: the health-care-industrial complex spends three times what the military-industrial complex spends in Washington."[22]

The health care lobby has even infiltrated the Senate Finance Committee, which is directly involved with health care legislation and programs. According to an analysis by the Lee Newspapers State Bureau in Montana, the health care lobby made campaign contributions totaling

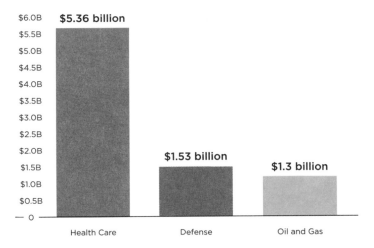

Lobbyist Spending Since 1998

Spending was between 1998 and 2012, according to Steven Brill, in a 2013 report, "Bitter Pill: Why Medical Bills are Killing Us"

$3.4 million from 2003-2008 to former Representative Max Baucus, a Montana Democrat who served as chairman of the committee. The ranking Republican committee member, Charles Grassley of Iowa, received $2.3 million in campaign contributions from the health care industry during that time period.[23]

Our country is $23 trillion in debt. Yet, the leadership of this country, the people who make the decisions regarding health care, are taking massive campaign contributions from the people who benefit from the current game. The health care industry should be embarrassed. It is responsible for sticking this nation with the highest health care costs in the world and providing some of the worst results while spending $5 billion lobbying Washington to keep the same crooked game in place. It gets even worse. Take a guess at what the CEOs of the top 70 publicly traded health care companies were paid, on average, for the years 2010-2017? Twenty million dollars of annual compensation, while Americans' health care system bankrupts the country with the worst results in the Western world.[24]

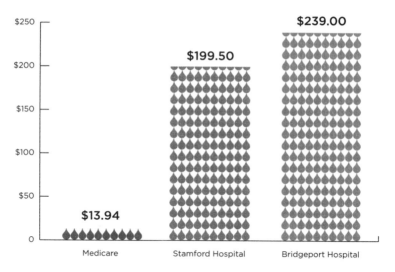

Blood Test Cost

As reported by journalist Steven Brill in 2013.

5. Health care pricing is a joke. If you purchase a cup of coffee at Starbucks or a turkey sandwich from Panera Bread, you will pay roughly the same price anywhere in the country. It's not the same with health care. As Brill reported, Medicare paid $13.94 for a blood test. For the same blood test, Stamford Hospital in Connecticut charged $199.50, and nearby Bridgeport Hospital charged $239. "More than $280 billion will be spent this year on prescription drugs in the United States," wrote Brill. "If we paid what other countries did for the same products, we would save $94 billion a year."[25] Yes, we could cut our deficit or invest in programs to the tune of $94 billion if we paid the same amount as other countries for drugs developed in the United States.

It gets worse. Our laws prevent the government from negotiating the best prices for Medicare. Imagine that. The government of the people, by the people, and for the people has laws in place that restrict it from negotiating the best possible drug prices for the people. Our politicians have created a game where the insurance companies and the drug companies win, and our citizens lose. The drug companies keep the politicians in office so that they can keep producing ridiculous profits. As a result, we pay far more for health care than anyone else in the world with the worst results, and no one is doing anything about it.

6. The health of the American people is poor. The numbers don't lie. The average American today weighs 30 pounds more than the average American weighed 60 years ago. We eat poorly and, as a whole, we don't exercise enough.[26] We are now the unhealthiest nation in the Western world, with nearly 40 percent of adults and 19 percent of our youth who are obese, according to the National Center for Health Statistics,[27] and the trend is likely to get even worse. Medical scientists say within 10 years, as many as 50 percent of Americans

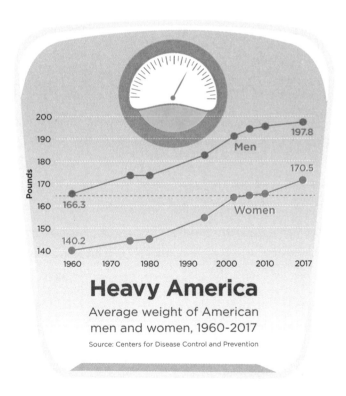

Heavy America

Average weight of American
men and women, 1960-2017

Source: Centers for Disease Control and Prevention

will be obese, and nearly one of every four of us will fall into the category of severely obese, according to the *New York Times* columnist Jane E. Brody.[28] During the two-year long debate about Obamacare, 99 percent of the conversation about health care centered around who gets covered and who pays the bill. The conversation did not include improving the overall health of the American people so that we don't have to spend the money on health care in the first place.

Here is an example of how ineffective our government has been at improving our health: "The Supplemental Nutrition Assistance Program (SNAP), which is funded by the government, pays for 20 million servings of sugary drinks a day, at an annual cost of $4 billion," a *New York Times* report said. "Barring recipients from using benefits to buy unhealthy beverages, researchers say, could prevent 52,000 deaths from Type 2 diabetes," said the 2019 article about a call to action from the American Academy of Pediatrics and the American Heart Association.[29] Yet our government does nothing.

Philadelphia started taxing soda 1.5 cents an ounce in 2017, and a study found that one year later, soda sales at major retail stores had fallen 38 percent.[30]

Why was there close to *zero* attention paid to the root cause of the problem? Because 40 percent of the voters are obese, and if you talk about what it really takes to reduce health care costs—which is unhealthy people taking personal responsibility for their health—you will lose votes. Unfortunately, our government leaders are in the business of getting reelected, not in the business of improving our country and dealing with the real problems that we have.

If I am elected your president, one of my top priorities will be to significantly improve the health of the American people. For those of you in poor health, I will do more for the health of you and your family than any other president in history. For those of you who are in good health, I will change the culture of our nation to value good health, and the cost of your health care will go down significantly over time.

Within the first 30 days of being in office, I will send to Congress the *Jack LaLanne Health Improvement Act of 2021* to honor one of our nation's earliest and greatest proponents of healthy living. LaLanne, a self-proclaimed junk food junkie until the age of 15, transformed himself into one of the nation's early fitness gurus.

LaLanne spent his life talking about the benefits of a healthy diet and exercise, and he strongly believed in taking responsibility for your health.

"Everything you do in life—I don't care, good or bad—don't blame God, don't blame the devil, don't blame me, blame you. You control everything! The thoughts you think, the words you utter, the foods you eat, the exercise you do. Everything is controlled by you," LaLanne said.[31]

It is my strong belief that if everyone in America took personal responsibility for their health, our health care costs would plummet and the quality of life in America would skyrocket. Watch the documentary *The Game Changers*,[32] and by the end, you will understand that people's diet is the number one factor in living a healthy life. If we want to be a great nation, we need to be a healthy nation. The key points of the *Jack LaLanne Health Improvement Act of 2021* will help all Americans improve their health and significantly reduce their costs over the long run:

1. Provide government health care for those who want it. There has been a debate in this country over the last 20 years regarding the government's role in the health of its citizens and participating in the costs. For those who don't like socialized medicine or a single-payer program, the reality is that we already have one. According to the Centers for Medicare and Medicaid Services, in 2019, 61.2 million people were enrolled in Medicare, the nation's health care program for the elderly, and 75.8 million were enrolled in Medicaid, the nation's health care program for the poor.[33] Added together, we now have more than 136 million Americans on a government health program. The *Jack LaLanne Health Improvement Act of 2021* will combine Medicare and Medicaid to create one national health program called Medicare 2.0. Medicare 2.0 will be our national health insurance platform to take care of those currently on Medicare, those on Medicaid, along with any American who needs health care. Those who currently have health insurance programs and are happy with their coverage will be able to keep those programs in place.

If you are on Medicare 2.0, your cost for insurance will be the following:

Income Level	Not Healthy		Healthy	
	Annual	Monthly	Annual	Monthly
Under $20,000	$600	$30	$0	$0
$20,000-$30,000	$1,200	$60	$600	$30
$30,000-$50,000	$2,400	$120	$1,200	$60
$50,000-$75,000	$4,800	$240	$2,400	$120
$75,000-$100,000	$7,200	$360	$3,600	$180
$100,000-$150,000	$9,600	$480	$4,800	$240
$150,000-$250,000	$12,000	$600	$6,000	$300
$250,000-$500,000	$16,000	$720	$8,000	$360
$500,000+	$20,000	$840	$10,000	$420

Medicare 2.0 accomplishes the following:

- Simplicity. We take two programs and make them one— Medicare 2.0. No Medicare and Medicaid. No Part A, Part B, Part C, Part D and M. A list of what is covered and what is not.

- Medicare 2.0 will take care of our poorest citizens. Many of our fellow citizens who are in financial difficulty and don't have the means to pay for insurance will be covered by Medicare 2.0.

- Medicare 2.0 gives a significant financial incentive to those who care about their bodies and live a healthy lifestyle. Those who score 750 or higher on the health risk assessment will pay lower prices.

- Significantly reduces health care costs. Medicare 2.0 acknowledges that the U.S. government is the biggest customer of the health care system in the United States. As part of the *Jack LaLanne Health Improvement Act*, the government will be allowed to negotiate all prices. I will put the best team in charge of Medicare 2.0, and it is my goal that we reduce costs by 20 percent by the 2024 fiscal year. This would result in a savings of over $268 billion a year, based on the most recent costs of the Medicare and Medicaid programs.

- Medicare 2.0 will put pressure on insurance companies to do a better job by increasing service and cutting costs. Americans spend more on health than any other country in the world because we spend $450 billion a year on insurance company coverage.[34] By eliminating most coverage from insurance companies and buying health care directly, we would recoup hundreds of billions of dollars. In addition to the cost savings, taking insurance companies out of the game would improve the care given to patients. Under the current system, insurance companies decide which tests and treatments they will cover for patients, often without talking to the patient or conducting a physical exam. In essence, the insurance companies practice medicine without a license. It is my hope that Medicare 2.0 will be a great program with amazing service and will cost significantly less than traditional health insurance. Over time, if Medicare 2.0 proves to be a better product at a lower cost than what insurance companies offer, more people and more companies will enroll, and the total health care costs will see a significant decline.

In addition to the financial case for Medicare 2.0, there is also a moral case. Too many Americans have significant health problems, through no fault of their own, and have no way to pay the bills.

A friend of mine had bone cancer in the 1970s. His leg had to be amputated to stop the cancer from spreading. His family was well off, and he was fitted with a prosthetic leg. A friend of his, whom he had met during his hospital stay, also had bone cancer and also lost a leg because of the disease but did not get an artificial limb. He asked his friend why not, thinking it might be because sometimes they hurt or can be difficult to use. His friend replied: "Because my parents can't afford it."

In another example, detailed by Elisabeth Rosenthal, editor in chief of Kaiser Health News, in a March 2017 article for *The New York Times Magazine*,[35] there's the story of Wanda Wickizer, who suffered a brain hemorrhage on Christmas Day 2013. She was flown by helicopter to the University of Virginia Medical Center in Charlottesville. After spending days in a coma, she slowly recovered. A widow who had temporarily quit working to care for her children, Wickizer, 51, had no insurance. The medical bills stacked up to $16,000 from Sentara Norfolk General Hospital (not including the scan or the emergency room doctor), $50,000 for the air ambulance, and $24,000 from the University of Virginia Physicians Group. She received a bill for $54,000 a month later from the same physicians group, which included further charges and late fees. Then the hospital bill came, amounting to nearly $357,000.

When the care providers called, insisting on payment of $285,507.58 —applying a 20 percent discount for uninsured patients—Wickizer explained that she didn't have that kind of money. She offered the hospital and its doctors $100,000 from her retirement account. They declined and suggested that she sign up for a payment plan of $5,000 per month to the hospital and $5,000 to the physicians. In October 2014, a sheriff affixed a summons to Wickizer's front door saying the university was suing her for nonpayment.

"In other countries, when patients recover from a terrifying brain bleed or, for that matter, when they battle cancer, or heal from a serious accident, or face down any other life-threatening health condition, they are allowed to spend their days focusing on getting better. Only in America do medical treatment and recovery coexist with a peculiar national dread: the struggle to figure out from the mounting pile of bills what portion of the fantastical charges you must pay," Rosenthal observed.

Americans should not have to worry about going to the hospital because of the costs, and they should not have to spend time arguing with insurance companies about whether they have coverage. We are the richest nation in the history of the world, and we should not tolerate this type of treatment for a fellow citizen in need. As a nation, we have a history of helping people when disaster strikes. We should follow our own example and have a health care system that takes care of people who, through no fault of their own, face financial ruin. My Medicare 2.0 proposal would take care of someone like Wanda Wickizer. If she were enrolled in Medicare 2.0, her costs would have been covered, and she would have been able to focus on her health and her family and would not have had to worry about her mounting bills, filing for bankruptcy, and being evicted from her house.

2. Create a Global Medical Response branch of the military. In 2015, after the Ebola outbreak, Microsoft cofounder Bill Gates gave a TED talk warning that a global pandemic even worse than Ebola would be likely to strike.[36] What Gates predicted in 2015 came to life with COVID-19 in 2020. Gates suggested in his 2015 speech that the world should form a medical reserve unit to monitor the world's health, develop plans to be prepared for any health crisis, and have a tool box at its disposal to quickly curb any potential pandemic. We have an awesome military that has incredible capabilities and can respond quickly to meet almost any threat. We need to have exactly the same thing for global health. If I am elected president, I would nominate Bill Gates to lead this effort and I would give him the budget necessary to get the job done and to make sure that we never see another global pandemic like COVID-19.

3. Implement the health risk assessment program for all Americans. What gets measured gets done, and if you opt in to be part of Medicare 2.0, you will be required to take a health risk assessment every year. This is a simple mini-physical that takes 20 minutes. Companies have successfully used health risk assessments, and they can help citizens check the current state of their health. The assessment can also help the government measure our progress toward becoming a healthy nation. If people do not want to participate, that is always an option, but failure to participate would mean that you will pay a higher price for Medicare 2.0. If the government is going to pay a portion of your health care, then you should be able to meet some simple expectations.

4. Institute a program where students from elementary school through high school take the health risk assessment and earn a grade for their health based on their score. This would be an effective way to get the attention of millions of students and families.

Health Risk Assessment Form

Biometric Category	Low	Points	Moderate Risk	Points	High Risk	Points
Total Cholesterol	< 200	50	200-239	25	≥ 240	0
HDL (women)	> 50	100	40-50	50	≤ 39	0
HDL (men)	> 40	100	35-40	50	≤ 34	0
LDL	≤ 129	50	130-159	25	≥ 160	0
TC/HDL Ratio	≤ 3.54	50	3.55-4.99	25	≥ 5.00	0
Triglycerides	≤ 149	100	150-199	50	≥ 200	0
Glucose	< 100	100	100-126	50	≥ 127	0
Blood Pressure (systolic)	< 130	100	130-139	50	≥ 14	0
Blood Pressure (diastolic)	< 85		85-89		≥ 90	0
Percent Body Fat (women)	< 28%	0	28%-32.9%	0	≥ 33%	0
Percent Body Fat (men)	< 22%	0	22%-27.9%	0	≥ 28%	0
BMI	< 25	50	25-29.9	25	≥ 30	0
Waist Circumference (women)	≤ 35	50	N/A	0	> 35	0
Waist Circumference (men)	≤ 40	50	N/A	0	> 40	0
Tobacco Use	Non-User	350	N/A	0	User	0

	Healthy Male	Unhealthy Male
Height	71"	70"
Weight	186 lbs.	243 lbs.
Blood pressure	103/62	140/96
Percent body fat	20.8%	32.7%
Body mass index	26	34.9
Waist circumference	35	45.5
Total cholesterol	166	231
Triglycerides	86	261
Glucose	85	135
Tobacco use	No	Yes
HRA POINT TOTAL	**950**	**150**

Source: www.MyInterraHealth.com

Kids care about their grades, and so do parents, and by making their actual health count as a class, it would bring focus toward achieving this goal. If children have a medical condition outside of their control, they can be exempt.

5. Basic nutritional information will be required on every food item that is for sale, whether it is in a restaurant, a grocery store, or at the ballpark. Americans need to know what they are consuming. Let's make sure that Americans clearly understand what they are eating all the time. In addition to nutritional information, the *Jack LaLanne Health Improvement Act* will require labeling on all sugary drinks, candies, and high-sugar content fast foods, warning that excess sugar consumption can cause diabetes and obesity—just as labels on cigarette packages warn that tobacco causes cancer. Diabetes is killing our citizens, and it costs us a fortune.

WARNING:
Drinking beverages with added sugar contributes to tooth decay, obesity, and diabetes.

A Baltimore councilman introduced legislation to require warning labels like this one on sugar-sweetened drinks in the city. A study published in Pediatrics found that such a label might deter parents from buying the drinks. Baltimore City Health Department

WARNING:
This product may cause mouth cancer.

WARNING:
This product may cause gum disease and tooth loss.

WARNING:
This product is not a safe alternative to cigarettes.
The Comprehensive Smokeless Tobacco Health Education Act of 1986 (Public Law 99-252) required three rotating warning labels on smokeless tobacco packaging and advertisements.

6. Health care-related companies will be prohibited from making campaign donations so that the health care—industrial complex cannot take advantage of the American people. This new legislation would prohibit donations from companies, unions, and political action committees. With this one move, we would prevent the insurance companies, drug companies, and others who make up the health care-industrial complex from creating a rigged game by buying elections with massive campaign contributions. We would free our representatives in Washington to vote for what is in the best interests of the American people, and not for what is in the best interests of the health care industry.

7. Publish health care results state by state, county by county. The Department of Health and Human Services will publish annual health rankings, including actual health scores from the health risk assessments and cost of health care, once a year, state by state, county by county. The rankings will create some local pride in becoming a healthy county. If we have a lot of healthy counties, we will have a lot of healthy states. If we have a lot of healthy states, we will have a healthy country. The rankings would help recognize the best-performing counties around the country, and they would also point out the worst-performing counties so the government could help those communities improve their health and spread best practices.

There is an amazing opportunity to improve the health of Americans, to increase life expectancy, and to drastically reduce the cost of our health care. As a nation, we cannot leave health care to the free market. It has not worked. The government can play a role in significantly reducing the cost of health care and improving the health of the American people. We don't leave the defense of this nation to private companies and to the market. This is especially urgent when you consider the fact that we currently spend almost 20 percent of our nation's GDP on health care, compared with about half that in most developed countries, and we get some of the worst results! The time has come to change the equation. Einstein said the definition of insanity is doing the same thing over and over again and expecting different results. As your president, I will provide the leadership to present the *Jack LaLanne Health Improvement Act of 2021* within my first 100 days, and I will do everything within my power to get this bill passed so we can improve the lives of hundreds of millions of Americans and significantly reduce our costs to avoid bankruptcy as a country.

In 2006 at Trek, we had three health-related events within two months. The first involved one of our truck drivers, who had a massive heart attack while driving across Iowa. The driver was a really good guy who was overweight and smoked. The heart attack cost Trek more than $500,000 and put an end to the driver's career. The second event happened to the spouse of one of our employees. Her husband worked for another company, had poor health habits, and was overweight. He suffered a stroke and never fully recovered, and their family has never been the same. The third event involved a manager in one of our warehouses. He was a great guy—a great big guy. I got a phone call one morning that he had died the night before. He was in his forties and had two young girls. A week later, I saw the death certificate. Cause of death? Obesity. That was the final straw for me.

I met with our human resources leader and told him that we could do better. I wanted to make some serious changes and boost the health of our employees. Later that week, I held an employee meeting and told the stories of what had happened over the past two months. I announced that we were going to make two specific changes to our health care plan: (1) we would require a health risk assessment every year, and (2) you had to reach a minimum score. If you did not meet that score, you needed to agree to take steps to improve your health by participating in programs sponsored by the company. Trek offers smoking cessation programs, nutritional counseling, on-site fitness classes, and on-site medical services that include counseling on weight, blood pressure and cholesterol. Failure to meet the minimum score or to participate in programs intended to address your health concerns would mean that you would pay a significantly higher share of your insurance.

My message was simple: We will give you one year to get on the program. We will provide seminars, individual coaching, smoking cessation assistance, and a fitness center. We will revamp our café to make sure that we have healthy options. But in the end, it is up to you.

I will tell you this: I had everyone's complete attention. I figured that there would be some upset employees afterward, and I was prepared to deal with that. To my surprise, I did not get one email. I did not get one employee visit on the topic.

We care about your health. If you do not care about your health, we are not going to pay for it.

What were the results? Let's take smoking. At the time, the national average of Americans who used tobacco products was over 20 percent; at Trek, the number was 22 percent. Today, 2.2 percent of Trek employees use tobacco. When we first started the health risk assessment program at Trek, our average score out of 1,000 points was a mediocre 772. Today, our average score is 901. We have significantly increased the health of employees at Trek because we were both compassionate and demanding. The biggest winners were the employees. Every year, we hold a dinner for employees who have worked at Trek for more than 20 years. The number one comment I get at the dinner is, "Thank you for the health care program. It has changed my life, and my getting healthy has improved the health of my spouse and my kids." Trek has not had a health plan cost increase in the last five years.

I have seen what has happened at Trek. Over the past five years, our health care costs have decreased, our employees are more productive, lead happier lives and have healthier kids. I know the same type of program can work in every company, every school, and many other organizations across the country. I also know that our government, which is paying the bill and setting the rules for health care in this country, could provide better leadership. If I am elected president, I will do everything in my power to pass the *Jack LaLanne Health Improvement Act of 2021*, and when that happens, the results will be amazing. It can be done! ●

5

Rebuild America

"President Eisenhower ... gave the nation its biggest construction project, the huge interstate-highway program that changed the shape of American society and made possible the expansion of the suburban middle class."

—James M. Perry, *The Wall Street Journal*, Oct. 27, 1995[1]

President Eisenhower challenged America to do something great by establishing the interstate highway system. Mostly built in the 1950s and 1960s, our transportation system was the envy of the world. It connected Americans from all over the country and drove commerce by making goods available and allowing them to flow freely and efficiently. Unfortunately, what was once the greatest transportation system in the world is today a system in steep decline. Our generation of political leaders has decided that it is more important to hold taxes down than to maintain a world-class transportation system.

If I am elected president, in my first month in office, I will send to Congress the *Eisenhower Two Transportation Act of 2021*. The proposed legislation will provide a blueprint for the American transportation system of the future and, most importantly, a way to pay for it.

If we, as a nation, want to have the most competitive economy in the world, we need to have the best transportation system in the world. To have the best transportation system in the world, we need to pay for it. As the saying goes, you get what you pay for. Other than Mexico, which has no gasoline tax, we have the lowest gas tax by far in the Western world,[2] and the condition of our transportation system is the worst. We are getting what we pay for.

The gas tax has not been raised since 1993,[3] while inflation has increased by 76.4 percent.[4] Since 1993, the U.S. population has grown by 69 million, or 27 percent,[5] and the number of vehicles registered has grown by 82 million, or 42 percent.[6] With more people driving more cars, and more bridges and roads to maintain, we are spending 76.4 percent less due to inflation. And we wonder why our transportation system is a mess. It is a mess because our leaders in Washington, D.C. do not have the political courage to fund good roads. They are more interested in staying in power by not increasing taxes than they are in making decisions in the best long-term interest of the country. The *Eisenhower Two Transportation Act* will increase the federal gas tax from the current 18.4 cents per gallon to $1 per gallon. Our political leaders have lacked the long-term thinking necessary to see the benefits of a world-class transportation system, and they have lacked the courage to pay for it by raising the gas tax.

The current tax on gasoline and diesel fuel generated $35 billion for our transportation needs in 2017, according to the Congressional Budget Office.[7] Based on that figure, the $1 per gallon gas tax would generate $190 billion per year and provide the funding necessary to transform our transportation system.

What facts describe our current transportation system?

1. Our nation's infrastructure is rated a D+ by the American Society of Civil Engineers.[8] This is an embarrassing grade for the largest economy in the world. Our roads, bridges, water pipes, airports, and railways are in sad shape. You can take a look at the studies and the numbers, and they are all bad. There is no one who says the transportation system in the United States is excellent. More importantly, you can drive around the country and see it everywhere: congestion, potholes, roads in terrible shape. Our highway system is falling apart as our leaders sit on their hands while the majority of the nations that we compete with pass us by. The infrastructures in Europe, China, and Japan are all superior to what we have in the United States. Following are key points from the American Society of Civil Engineers' 2017 Infrastructure Report Card:

- As a result of years of inadequate funding, the nation's roads and bridges have a backlog of $836 billion worth of repairs, expansion, and enhancements needed.

- Roads merited a D grade. The report says of the more than four million miles of roads across the nation, one of every five miles of highway is in poor shape, and the battered pavement cost motorists an extra $120.5 billion in additional vehicle repairs and operating costs in 2015, amounting to $533 per driver.

- Of 16 types of infrastructure assessed, all but four—rail, bridges, ports, and solid waste—netted a D+ or worse.

- Bridges earned a C+, but of more than 614,000 bridges nationwide, 56,000, or 9.1 percent, were structurally deficient in 2016, and vehicles made 188 million trips across them every day. Nearly four out of every 10 bridges are at least 50 years old.

- Thanks to improvements by the private freight rail industry, which owns the majority of the U.S. railroad infrastructure, the rail system was rated a B grade. But investments in passenger rail have not kept pace with the growing need, and Amtrak's busy Northeast Corridor between Boston and Washington, D.C., where ridership topped 30 million in 2016, needs $28 billion worth of updates and repairs.

Infrastructure Report Card

Category	1988*	1998	2001	2005	2009	2013	2017
Aviation	B-	C-	D	D+	D	D	D
Bridges	—	C-	C	C	C	C+	C+
Dams	—	D	D	D+	D	D	D
Drinking Water	B-	D	D	D-	D-	D	D
Energy	—	—	D+	D	D+	D+	D+
Hazardous Waste	D	D-	D+	D	D	D	D+
Inland Waterways	B-	—	D+	D-	D-	D-	D
Levees	—	—	—	—	D-	D-	D
Ports	—	—	—	—	—	C	C+
Public Parks & Recreation	—	—	—	C-	C-	C-	D+
Rail	—	—	—	C-	C-	C+	B
Roads	C+	D-	D+	D	D-	D	D
Schools	D	F	D-	D	D	D	D+
Solid Waste	C-	C-	C+	C+	C+	B-	C+
Transit	C-	C-	C-	D+	D	D	D-
Wastewater	C	D+	D	D-	D-	D	D+
GPA	**C**	**D**	**D+**	**D**	**D**	**D+**	**D+**
Cost to Improve**	—	—	$1.3T	$1.6T	$2.2T	$3.6T	$4.59T

*The first infrastructure grades were given by the National Council on Public Works Improvements in its report Fragile Foundations: A Report on America's Public Works, released in February 1988. ASCE's first Report Card for America's Infrastructure was issued a decade later.

**The 2017 Report Card's investment needs are over 10 years. The 2013 Report is over eight years. In the 2001, 2005, and 2009 Report Cards the time period was five years.

- Drinking water, carried through one million miles of pipes, got a D grade. Many of the pipes were installed in the early to mid-20th century with an expected lifespan of 75 to 100 years. The American Water Works Association says $1 trillion is needed to maintain and expand service over the next 25 years.

- In all, it would take $4.6 trillion to fix the entire U.S. infrastructure system by 2025, the ASCE says.

2. Our roads are not as safe as they should be. In 2018, we had over 40,000 deaths and 4.5 million serious injuries on our roads.[9] As many as 14,000 motorists die every year due to poor road conditions.[10] Americans should be outraged.

3. Good infrastructure drives the economy. The transportation system does not just matter when you are going from point A to point B in your car. The transportation system provides services that support economic growth by increasing the productivity of workers and capital. The better our transportation system, the better our economy will be.

The gas tax is a simple solution to fix the transportation system in the United States. The gas tax has funded transportation projects since 1932[11] and, at one point in time, created the greatest transportation system in the world. For some reason, our leaders decided it was more important to keep the gas tax down than it was to maintain a world-class transportation system. We got exactly that: A low gas tax and a transportation system in major decline.

If I am elected president, I will do what no other president has done in the last 25 years by proposing a major increase in the gas tax so we can significantly improve our transportation system and pay for it at the same time. Other countries have figured out how to use the gas tax to fund their transportation systems.

Some people in Washington have proposed raising the gas tax by 15 cents, and it has been defeated every time. Boosting the gas tax to $1 per gallon is a simple and bold plan that would create the revenue necessary to rebuild our crumbling transportation system, improve our economy by speeding the flow of goods, put millions of Americans to work in high-paying construction jobs, and save thousands of lives every year.

A $1 per gallon gas tax would still leave our combined federal and average state gas tax at less than 50 percent of the rates in Germany, the U.K., and most other Western nations.[12]

This plan makes sense because of the following:

1. It is simple. The gas tax already funds the country's transportation system. The simplest solution is to use the same approach. The gas tax is effective. The people who use the roads pay for the roads, and this eliminates many of the complaints associated with other taxes. Ronald Reagan once said, "Good tax policy decrees that, wherever possible, a fee for a service should be assessed against those who directly benefit from that service."[13]

2. It will make mass transit more accessible. Nearly 45 percent of Americans lack access to mass transit,[14] and a major trend is that young people are driving less and using other modes of transportation more. A $1 per gallon gas tax will provide the funds necessary to develop alternative modes of transportation for the majority of Americans who are living in cities.

3. The future of transportation is changing. Autonomous vehicles will have a significant impact on our transportation system over the next 20 years. This will increase the competitiveness of our economy and increase our standard of living, but only if we make the needed investments in our infrastructure. The *Eisenhower Two Transportation Act* will be able to fund the rebuilding of America's infrastructure so future technologies can be deployed in America.

Some will say the *Eisenhower Two Transportation Act* is a major tax increase that Americans cannot afford. I believe that as a nation, we cannot afford *not* to address our crumbling transportation system, and we need to provide the funds to pay for it instead of continuing to heap additional debt on the backs of future generations of Americans. Those at the lower end of the income range will be able to afford this because of other proposed changes, including a higher minimum wage and significantly lower medical costs.

We cannot be the greatest nation in the world or have the best economy in the world if we have the worst transportation system. If I am elected president, the *Eisenhower Two Transportation Act* will allow us to make more progress in rebuilding America's transportation system in four years than we have made in the past 40 years. The *Eisenhower Two Transportation Act* will leave our children with a better transportation system than we currently have and will give our children a better chance to compete in the future global marketplace.

The future of our transportation system matters, and if I am elected president, I will provide the plan and the leadership to get the job done. ✔

6

Increase Opportunity in America

"How can we love our country and not love our countrymen, and loving them, reach out a hand when they fall, heal them when they are sick, and provide opportunities to make them self-sufficient so they will be equal in fact and not just in theory?"

—Ronald Reagan[1]

O ne of the greatest things about the United States is the belief anyone can succeed. There are countless rags-to-riches stories in America. Every American should have the opportunity to rise up the socioeconomic ladder based on intelligence and hard work. Unfortunately, over the last 30 years, inequality in America has risen, and the ability to move from rags to riches has diminished. Historically, part of the beauty of America has been a strong middle class. Yale economist and Nobel Prize winner Robert J. Shiller called the rising economic inequality "the most important problem that we are facing now today."[2] Former Federal Reserve Board chairman Alan Greenspan said, "This is not the type of thing which a democratic society—a capitalist democratic society—can really accept without addressing,"[3] and President Obama has referred to the widening income gap as the "defining challenge of our time."[4]

A study led by Harvard University business professor Michael Porter shows that prosperity hinges on opportunity: "A nation is competitive if it creates the conditions where two things occur simultaneously: businesses operating in the nation can (1) compete successfully in domestic and international markets, while (2) maintaining and improving the wages and living standards of the average citizen. When these occur together, a nation prospers. When one occurs without the other, a nation is not truly competitive and prosperity is not sustainable."[5]

What we have in the United States today are companies that are competing successfully in the domestic market and international markets. The problem we have is that we are failing on Porter's second point. Wages and the living standard for the average citizen are not improving. Over time, if the middle class continues to evaporate, and if the wealth gap continues to grow, the prosperity that we have enjoyed as a nation will diminish, and our form of government will be at risk.

What evidence exists that the income gap is a serious issue in America?

- **America's famous middle class is shrinking, and the income gap between rich and poor is growing.** From 1950 to 1980, the top 1 percent of income earners received 10 percent of the country's pre-tax income. By 2012, their share of pre-tax income had jumped to 23 percent.[6] While the top 1 percent has been accumulating more wealth, the bottom 50 percent has seen its share of pre-tax income almost cut in half, from 20 percent to 12.5 percent.[7] The Pew Research Center, in a 2018 report, showed the share of adults with a middle-class income was 61 percent in 1971. By 2016, that number had fallen to 52 percent.[8]

- **One of every eight Americans—or nearly 12 percent of us— live in poverty, according to U.S. Census data**[9]. Would you have guessed that? What's worse is in this country there are just under 13 million children who are living in poverty, and about half of their families are below 50 percent of the poverty line. Of 38 nations surveyed by the Organization for Economic Cooperation and Development, only nine other countries had a higher rate of children living in poverty than the United States.[10]

- **We are the most powerful nation in history, and yet we rank tenth highest in child poverty.** How can our government plan to spend $1.2 trillion over the next 30 years modernizing our nuclear weapons program, but it cannot address the issue of childhood poverty? When was the last time you heard a candidate running for the presidency talk about childhood poverty?

Nearly 13 million children
lived in poverty in 2018 and

about half of them
in households earning less
than 50% of the poverty line

Child Poverty Rates in These Countries

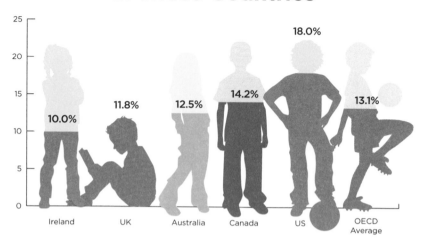

Why do we have such a large wealth gap in the United States? And why is it getting larger? This is a complicated issue, but there are three major factors.

First, globalization has created a "winner takes all" environment. Talented companies and individuals are able to go global. This is great for the few who can play on the global stage, but not so good for those who play only on the local stage. Take the iPhone, an amazing global product. Because of globalization, Apple can sell iPhones worldwide and dominate the market. Thirty years ago, different companies would have been making phones for each country.

The second major factor is technology. The iPhone has more power and capabilities than the systems that took Apollo 11 to the moon. Computers have increased the quality of life, but they have also wiped out millions of well-paying jobs. Fewer factory workers are needed to build products, fewer accountants are needed to keep track of companies' books, and fewer customer service people are needed to help at the airport. Because of the computer, the world has become more efficient, but fewer of the traditional jobs of past generations are now available.

The third major factor that has contributed to inequality is the U.S tax policy. Starting around 1980, the tax code became much more favorable for those at the top of the ladder. The favorable tax policy for the wealthy in this country continued with the Trump tax cuts. The average person in the top 1 percent received a tax cut of $34,000, while a person in the bottom 10 percent got a tax cut of $50.[11]

I believe it is important for the people of the United States to address the growing disparity between rich and poor and a shrinking middle class for the following reasons:

1. We are losing the knowledge and skills of a lot of people who do not have hope for a brighter future. Millions of Americans have given up. The lack of a fair chance costs this country potentially billions of dollars from those who have lost hope. Historically, the growing middle class has provided hope, opportunities, and an incentive for many Americans to climb the ladder.

2. The large inequality gap puts tremendous pressure on the government to take care of people who cannot afford to take care of themselves. The result is increased government spending. Those who are doing well should be fearful of the future. If a large segment of society has no hope for the future, and if that trend continues, then the few at the top will not last. History tells us that eventually, the people will revolt. This could happen in the United States in the not-so-distant future.

3. We have a history in our country of taking care of those who cannot help themselves. Social Security, the minimum wage, the GI Bill, Medicare, Medicaid—all great programs that our government created to make an investment to help people help themselves. Do we want to undo any of these programs?

It is in the best interest of every American to strive for a society and an economy that rewards hard work and provides the opportunity for everyone who wants to climb the economic ladder. As a country, we need to recognize that the numbers are telling us the opposite is happening, and if we want a different result, we need to make major changes. We are the richest nation on Earth, and we should be embarrassed by the growing economic inequality in our society.

Within the first 100 days of my administration, I will propose the *War on Poverty Act of 2021,* containing four specific proposals that will make sure the middle class in this country is rebuilt, and every American who wants to work hard has a fair chance in the future:

1. Increase the minimum wage to $15 per hour—now. The current federal minimum wage of $7.25 doesn't cut it. This wage adds up to just $15,000 per year. A family cannot pay rent, feed themselves, buy clothing, and buy insurance for $15,000 per year. By raising the federal minimum wage to $15 per hour, those most in need would receive more money from their jobs. It is far better to receive money from the marketplace in the form of higher compensation than a handout from the government in the form of welfare.

2. Create the *Every Kid Has a Chance Program* with the goal of reducing childhood poverty by 50 percent in the next 10 years. Charles M. Blow, in a 2015 column in *The New York Times,* called America's child poverty level "unconscionable."[12]

"People may disagree about the choices parents make—including premarital sex and out-of-wedlock births. People may disagree about access to methods of family planning—including contraception and abortion. People may disagree about the size and role of government—including the role of safety-net programs.

But surely we can all agree that no child, once born, should suffer through poverty. Surely we can all agree that working to end child poverty—or at least severely reduce it—is a moral obligation of a civilized society.

There are about 13 million American children who live in poverty. Six million of those children come from homes that receive Social Security benefits."

Within the *War on Poverty Act of 2021*, I will include legislation to create the *Every Kid Has a Chance Program*. For those kids whose families are below 50 percent of the poverty level, the government will offer a simple program to provide:

- Three basic meals a day until the age of 22
- Free basic Medicare until the age of 22
- Free education until the age of 22

The *Every Kid Has a Chance Program* would take a giant step in giving the poorest children in our society a chance in life, and it would create productive, taxpaying citizens for the future. It would also give kids at the bottom of the socioeconomic ladder, along with their families, hope for the future.

Imagine the long-term cost difference for a kid born in poverty who stays in poverty, ends up in jail, goes through the legal system, and winds up on welfare compared to the kid who is born into poverty, through no fault of his or her own, and is guaranteed three basic meals a day, health care, and a free education. Over the long haul, which program makes more sense for our country in terms of dealing with childhood poverty? Our current system? Or the *Every Kid Has a Chance Program*? Which program holds the higher moral ground? Which program costs less over the long term? This is an opportunity for government to help people who cannot help themselves and save money for every American taxpayer in the long run by producing more productive, taxpaying citizens for the future.

3. Have the Department of Education offer to take over the poorest performing 1 percent of public schools in the country. Education matters. American children hold the key to our future, whether they are rich or poor. In our country, the rich kids are taken care of by better schools and by parents who have the resources to raise productive citizens of the future. I know this. I was born with two amazing parents and have lived a great life. I have mentored some kids who were born poor, with tough family situations, and I have watched the cycle of poverty destroy futures and destroy hope.

Chief Justice Earl Warren wrote in the 1954 Brown v. Board of Education ruling, "It is doubtful that any child may reasonably be expected to succeed in life if he is denied the opportunity of an education. Such an opportunity, where the state has undertaken to provide it, is a right which must be made available to all on equal terms."[13]

The reality in America today is that our children who are born into poverty do not have the equal opportunity that Chief Justice Warren wrote about. The vast majority of kids born into poverty can't get out. As *The Atlantic* reported, students in higher-income towns in Connecticut, such as Greenwich and Darien, have easy access to guidance counselors, school psychologists, personal laptops, and up-to-date textbooks that those in high-poverty areas, like Bridgeport and New Britain, do not.[14] Such districts tend to have more students in need of extra help, and yet they have fewer guidance counselors, tutors, and psychologists. They have lower-paid teachers, more dilapidated facilities, and bigger class sizes than wealthier districts, according to a lawsuit. Greenwich spends $6,000 more per pupil per year than Bridgeport does, according to the state's Department of Education. *The Atlantic* article notes a landmark 2013 report from a group convened by the former Education Secretary Arne Duncan, the Equity and Excellence Commission, which concluded, "Our system does not distribute opportunity equitably."[15]

For the most part, children below 50 percent of the poverty line come from disadvantaged or single-parent households, with limited or no financial resources, and attend the nation's worst schools. Within the *War on Poverty Act*, my administration will propose to Congress that states are given the opportunity to cede control of any of their schools in the poorest performing 1 percent to the Department of Education. The states would give the Department of Education the amount of money that they are spending on these schools. The Department of Education will put together a SEAL Team-like division with a high sense of urgency to take control of these schools and turn them around fast so the poorest children in our country can have a realistic chance of becoming productive, taxpaying citizens of the future.

These schools, if we are successful, will serve as examples for other schools in low-income areas. If this test succeeds, then I will propose to Congress that the program be expanded. If this program fails, I will propose that the program be shut down. I am a strong believer in looking at problems, trying new things, keeping what works, and getting rid of what doesn't. Above all, I am for doing something!

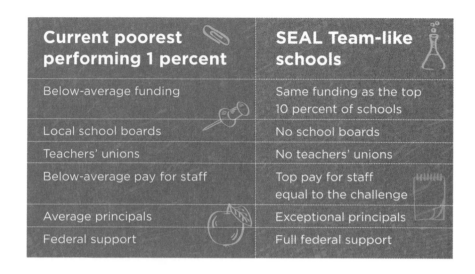

Current poorest performing 1 percent	SEAL Team-like schools
Below-average funding	Same funding as the top 10 percent of schools
Local school boards	No school boards
Teachers' unions	No teachers' unions
Below-average pay for staff	Top pay for staff equal to the challenge
Average principals	Exceptional principals
Federal support	Full federal support

As noted earlier, Einstein said insanity is doing the same thing over and over again and expecting a different result. We have been running the same play in our worst public schools for decades. We get the same pathetic results. Let's do something different.

My administration will not run and hide from our worst schools. We will take the opposite approach and adopt these schools. We will use overwhelming force to take our most at-risk kids and give them the education they need and the education they deserve.

If this program is successful, I will come back to Congress and ask that the federal government continue to take over the administration of more of our nation's poorest performing schools until the day comes when we can say that all children in the United States have access to an excellent education.

4. Scrap the cap on Social Security taxes. How do we pay for the *War on Poverty Act of 2021*? The usual way the government pays for a new program is to add it to our deficit. I believe we need to be fiscally prudent, and the proper way to pay for the *War on Poverty Act* is to scrap the cap on Social Security taxes. The current program mandates that you pay a percentage of your income into Social Security up to a certain amount. In 2019, that percentage is 6.2, and the amount is $132,900.[16] So, for example, someone who makes $80,000 a year pays $4,960 in Social Security taxes. Yet someone who makes $10 million, or 172 times that amount, only has to pay approximately $8,240. By scrapping the Social Security cap, the person with $10 million in earnings would pay $620,000. Scrapping the cap would secure Social Security for the future and would pay for the *War on Poverty Act*.

By increasing the minimum wage to $15 an hour, launching a war on childhood poverty through the *Every Kid Has a Chance Program*, experimenting with SEAL Team-like schools, and paying for these programs by scrapping the cap on Social Security, we would give hope to an entire generation of Americans who live at the bottom of the ladder.

As a nation, we have made very little progress in reducing economic inequality over the past 30 years. If I am elected, my administration will implement new policies to deliver different results. We have the ability to increase fairness in our society and enhance the American Dream for generations to come. It can be done! ●

7

Reform Congress

"All members of Congress should be required to wear NASCAR uniforms. You know, the kind with patches. That way we know who is sponsoring each of them."

—Brad Thor, best selling author[1]

Ask anyone which of our three branches of government has been the most ineffective over the past 20 years, and the likely answer is Congress. Congress has an average approval rating of around 20 percent over the last 10 years and a deservedly poor reputation.[2]

Let's take a look at how bad Congress is and why it needs to be fixed:

1. Congress is in charge of our nation's pocketbook. Not a dime can be spent without the approval of Congress, other than an executive order by the president. We have a national debt of over $23 trillion,[3] which translates to roughly $66,800 for every American. Congress has primary responsibility for this—not the president.

2. Congress failed to pass a budget for 1,448 days between 2009–2013.[4] Imagine any business in America, let alone the largest business in America, that does not have a budget. Our Congress is so dysfunctional that we went almost four years without a budget.

3. Money has a major influence in Congress from start to finish. The average U.S. Senate campaign in 2016 cost $10.4 million. When you add outside spending, the actual cost was $19.4 million.[5] In 2018, 91 percent of candidates running for a seat in the House and 84 percent of Senate contenders who outspent their opponents during their campaigns won their respective elections.[6] One of the major problems with Congress is that it is awash with money, yet Congress has done basically nothing to address campaign finance reform. From 1998 to 2004, 43 percent of retiring members of Congress took lobbying jobs after they left Congress.[7] That number is up from 3 percent in 1974.[8] Why are so many members of Congress turning into lobbyists? Because corporations are willing to pay them to lobby their former colleagues to influence legislation that might be worth hundreds of millions or billions of dollars.

As one example, former Representative Billy Tauzin (R-LA) made almost $20 million as a lobbyist for the pharmaceutical industry between 2006 and 2010, according to the *New York Daily News.*[9] During Tauzin's time in Congress, where he served from 1980–2005, he helped pass President Bush's prescription drug expansion. As a well-paid lobbyist, his association helped to block a proposal to allow Medicare to negotiate drug prices. That proposal, had it passed, would have saved American taxpayers billions of dollars. The high salaries that lobbying firms are paying former members of Congress are actually cheap. Our democracy is for sale, and there is no better example of our government being for sale than Congress.

We all have a vested interest in making sure that Congress is an effective branch of our government. If I am elected president, I will propose the *Congressional Reform Act of 2021* within the first 100 days of my administration. The following points will form the basis of the *Congressional Reform Act of 2021*, which, if passed, would make Congress significantly more productive than it is today and will be in the best interest of all Americans:

1. Change the terms and install term limits. We don't need career-long members of Congress—that's clearly not working. The 22nd Amendment states that the president can serve two four-year terms. Let's take an idea that is already working and send it down Pennsylvania Avenue to Congress. Members of the Senate and the House of Representatives should hold four-year terms, as well, instead of two years for representatives and six years for senators.

I will ask Congress to pass a constitutional amendment to change both Senate and House seats to four-year terms, and put a two-term cap on their potential service, giving them no more than eight years in office. Half of Congress would be up for election every two years to make sure our government changes with the times. Here are the potential benefits:

- The idea of the "career politician" would cease if the maximum amount of time that anyone could serve in Congress were eight years.

- Campaign spending would be reduced. Much of the money that flows into campaigns goes to candidates who have been in office for many years and have a lot of power because of their tenure.

Money flows to power, and the longer you serve, the more power you have. The more power you have, the more money you get. This ends up being a vicious circle, and it has been demonstrated in our Congress.

- Term limits would take power from career politicians and those who fund their campaigns and send it back to the people they are serving.

- Members of Congress would begin to focus on solving the nation's problems instead of running for reelection. Today's politicians spend as much as 50 percent of their time raising money for the next election, up from 10 to 15 percent in the 1980s and 1990s, said Nick Penniman, CEO of Issue One, which describes itself as a "crosspartisan" political reform group.[10] By putting term limits in place, we would significantly reduce the amount of time politicians spend raising money, allowing our nation's elected officials the ability to spend more time solving the problems of the nation.

- The quality of political candidates would improve. By imposing term limits, we are more likely to attract political candidates who are interested in serving their country, not in creating a career.

2. Change the pay and benefits for members of Congress.
The *Congressional Reform Act of 2021* will propose that if a member of Congress has a net worth of more than $10 million, he or she should not receive compensation. That would affect 46 members of the House and the Senate, as of February 2018.[11] Such powerful positions should represent what our Founding Fathers intended— public service rather than a career with excellent pay and benefits. Members of Congress with a net worth of less than $10 million should be entitled to current compensation and expenses.

In addition, I will propose that the pension program for Congress be terminated. Under the current system, senators and representatives can pull in a pension at age 62 if they have held office for at least five years, or at age 50 if they have served in Congress for 20 years. As of October 2018, there were 619 retired members of Congress getting pensions, according to the Congressional Research Service. Just over half of them were paid an average of $75,528 a year through an older program that didn't include Social Security. The others, covered by a newer pension program that includes Social Security, got $41,208 a year, on average. That totals $36.3 million that the government spent on Congressional pensions, just in 2018.[12]

Congress survived without a pension program until the 1940s, and with our current financial state, we should not be paying members of Congress a pension. I don't believe that applying these rules would result in less-qualified individuals running for Congress. In fact, I believe that we will get a better group of people interested in the job. The benefits of making these changes would include the following:

- The message would be clear that the U.S. government is built on public service, and those who rise to the occasion are making a sacrifice and serving their country.

- We would enjoy tremendous cost savings. This solution would save the United States at least $44 million per year in salary and pension payments.

3. Eliminate the filibuster. A filibuster is a political procedure where one or more members of Congress stages a long debate over a proposed piece of legislation to delay or entirely prevent a decision from being made on the proposal. It is sometimes referred to as "talking a bill to death" or "talking out a bill" and is characterized as a form of obstruction in a legislature or other decision-making body. The filibuster can force any controversial proposal in the Senate to require 60 of the 100 Senate votes, meaning that not even a simple majority can carry the day and that a group of 41 senators can block

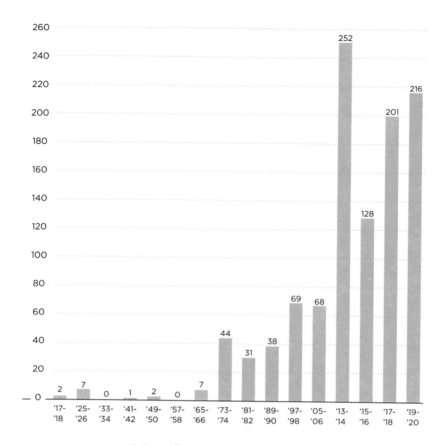

Motion Sickness

Number of motions filed to end a filibuster
in each two-year session of Congress

Source: United States Senate. https://www.senate.gov/legislative/cloture/clotureCounts.htm

any legislation. The impact of the filibuster has been massive. For example, our inability to confront major issues like gun violence and climate change is partially due to the filibuster. As a nation, we have big problems that need to be solved, and the Senate should abolish the filibuster and allow the majority to carry the day.

4. Give the president the line-item veto. Congress has put our nation into debt to the tune of $23 trillion. Congress rarely passes clean bills to be signed. When the president signs a bill, it usually comes with numerous unrelated, unnecessary, political back-scratching add-ons. As a check and balance, the president should have the ability to protect the American taxpayer. Currently, 45 state governors have a line-item veto.[13] It is time that we give this power to the president, whether he or she is a Democrat or a Republican or an Independent. The line-item veto will be part of the *Congressional Reform Act* that I send to Congress.

The Gerrymandering of Maryland's Third District

83rd Congress
1953-1955

113th
2013-2015

The Gerrymandering of Pennsylvania's Seventh District

83rd Congress
1953-1955

113th
2013-2015

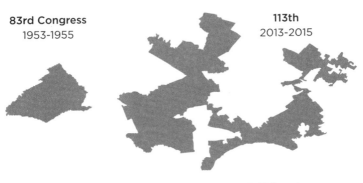

Source: Shapefiles maintained by Jeffrey B. Lewis, Brandon DeVine, Lincoln Pritcher and Kenneth C. Martis, UCLA. Drawn to scale.

5. End gerrymandering. I will ask Congress, as part of the *Congressional Reform Act*, to eliminate gerrymandering—the practice of redrawing congressional districts for the sole purpose of benefiting one political party—and have non-partisan, independent commissions put in charge of drawing districts. By putting an end to gerrymandering, less extreme candidates will have a better chance of success and so will compromise. For examples of how politicians have rigged the game by changing the borders of their districts to increase their odds of reelection, look no further than Maryland and Pennsylvania. A federal judge said Maryland's Third District map looked like "a broken-winged pterodactyl,"[14] while David Daley, publisher of *The Connecticut Mirror*, described Pennsylvania's Seventh District as Goofy kicking Donald Duck.[15] Both states were ordered to redraw the district borders.

We cannot have a better government without a better Congress, and Congress has shown no inclination over the years to improve itself. These five simple recommendations will lead to a more efficient, more productive Congress and a body more representative of the people's needs. I am not running for president because I believe we need small change. I am running for president because I think we need to improve all aspects of our government, including Congress. We deserve better. ✔

8

Cut Defense Spending

"Every gun that is made, every warship
launched, every rocket fired signifies in the
final sense, a theft from those who hunger
and are not fed, those who are cold
and are not clothed."

—Dwight D. Eisenhower[1]

Throughout our history, the American military has kept our nation safe and preserved our liberty and our way of life. Millions have served, and many of our fellow countrymen have paid the ultimate price. Along with our Allies, our military succeeded in saving Europe in World War I and virtually the entire world in World War II. Our military oversaw the end of the Cold War, and most recently, our military personnel, along with our Allies, have been laying their lives on the line for the War on Terror in the Middle East.

Every American owes a debt of gratitude to the men and women who have served in our armed forces. As with anything, times change, and as a nation, we must realize that we spend more money on defense than we can afford. This opinion has nothing to do with questioning the men and women who have served in the military; it has everything to do with the recognition that we have a $23 trillion debt, and to solve it, we need to put every expense on the table, including how much money we spend in the Department of Defense.

How much money do we spend defending our country? That depends on how you want to count. I am reminded of the story of two people who interview with a CEO to become the chief financial officer of a company. The CEO asks a final question of both candidates: What is one plus one? The first candidate answers, "Two." The second candidate answers, "Whatever you want it to be." Accounting can be tricky, especially if you are talking about accounting for the Defense Department. Here is a summary of how much money we are currently spending as a nation on defense in our 2020 budget:

Base level of spending	$633.3 billion
Contingency funding for wars fought overseas	$71.3 billion
Subtotal	**$704.6 billion**[2]

Additional spending by agencies that protect America:

Department of Veterans Affairs	$220.6 billion[3]
Homeland Security	$50.5 billion[4]
FBI and national security	$10.0 billion[5]
National nuclear security	$16.7 billion[6]
Overseas contingency funding for state and homeland security	$8.2 billion
Grand total:	**$1.0 trillion**

If I am elected president, I will put all of our military expenditures in one budget so that we will provide transparency for those who are making decisions and for those who are paying the bill—the American taxpayer. I will work with our military to come up with a plan to reduce total defense-related expenditures from $1 trillion to $850 billion in fiscal 2022 and $750 billion in fiscal 2023. This would be a reduction of $250 billion. Admiral Mike Mullen, the former chairman of the Joint Chiefs of Staff, has said, "The greatest threat to our national security is our debt."[7] Our current military budget is one of the main reasons why we have such a large debt. Here are some facts that illustrate just how big of a spending problem we have in the Department of Defense:

1. In 2019, the United States made up 4.3 percent of the world's population[8], yet we were responsible for 35.6 percent of the publicized, global military expenditures. We spend more money on defense than the next eight countries combined, according to the Stockholm International Peace Research Institute.[9]

Playing Defense

Defense spending by country

Spending in Billions (estimate)

TOTAL SPENDING: **$655.4 Billion**   TOTAL SPENDING: **$704.6 Billion**

China: **$250 Billion**

Saudi Arabia: **$67.6 Billion**

India: **$66.5 Billion**

France: **$63.8 Billion**

Russia: **$61.4 Billion**

United Kingdom: **$50 Billion**

Germany: **$49.5 Billion**

Japan: **$46.6 Billion**

$704.6 Billion
United States

Source: Stockolm International Peace Research Institute, SIPRI Military Expenditure Database April 2015. Data 2014. Compiled by PGPF. Note: Figures are in U.S. dollars, converted from local currencies using market exchange rates.

U.S. costs shown here reflect 2018 budget for Department of Defense only.

2. The Department of Defense has three different budgets: a baseline budget, plus two "supplemental" budgets. If a particular item misses the first budget, it always has a second and even third chance.[10]

3. The American military has many duplicative efforts that result in massive costs. For example, the United States maintains two ground forces (the Army and Marine Corps) and four air forces (the Air Force, Marine Corps aviation, Naval Air Forces, and the CIA's fleet of aircraft and drones).

4. We have more military bases around the world than we need, but we do not have the political courage to shut them down. In addition to all of the military bases inside the United States, the Defense Department operates about 800 bases overseas with personnel in 80 nations.[11] We do not need all of these bases, but no one has the political courage to propose that we close the bases that we do not need.

Military Bases

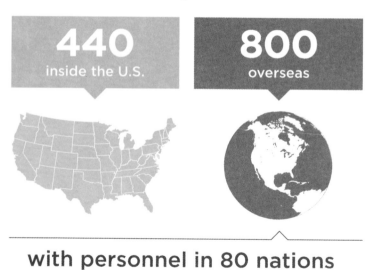

440 inside the U.S.

800 overseas

with personnel in 80 nations

5. The United States Defense Department's weapons program is massive and inefficient. Currently, weapons are designed to be built in key congressional districts; they are not designed to be built in the most efficient manner.

One example is the F-22 fighter jet program, which had over 1,000 suppliers in 46 states.[12] Members of Congress use their influence to push the Pentagon to appoint suppliers in their districts even when those suppliers add to the cost and complexity of the program. Then those same companies that received the work, based on politics, make large donations to the same member of Congress to keep the contract.

According to OpenSecrets.org, defense contractors gave members of the Armed Services panel almost $10 million in the 2016 election cycle. Rep. Mac Thornberry (R-Texas), the chair of the House Armed Services Committee, netted nearly $394,000—the most money from the sector of any member of Congress. He even bested all of the 2016 presidential candidates, except Hillary Clinton who received over $1 million, and Bernie Sanders, who received almost $418,000.[13]

The Pentagon, which is in charge of the Department of Defense budget, cannot do its job of providing the best weapons systems at the most competitive price because Congress is playing politics. The political game that Congress plays with the Department of Defense sourcing is costing the nation billions of dollars.

There are a number of members of Congress who, in an effort to benefit their districts, have pushed to spend money on military projects the Pentagon does not even want. One example is the production of M-1 tanks. In March 2012, U.S. Army Chief of Staff General Raymond Odierno told the House Appropriations Committee that the Army did not need new tanks and that the tanks it had did not need to be upgraded until 2017. The Army and Marine Corps had 6,000 tanks in inventory at that time. Only 1,000 were used in the Iraqi war.[14]

The Army and the Marines were trying to make a decision in the best long-term interest of the country. Unfortunately, by canceling the M-1 tanks, a large factory in Lima, Ohio, would have been idled, and subcontractors in Pennsylvania, Michigan, and other key states would have been affected, as well. General Dynamics, a defense supplier that has donated millions of dollars to congressional elections over the past decade, mobilized its supporters and saved the M-1.[15]

Another example of a weapons program that has spiraled out of control is the F-35 being built by Lockheed Martin, the most expensive weapons system in U.S. history. In 2016, as the project was running seven years behind schedule and already had run up a cost of more than $400 billion—almost twice the initial estimate—Senator John McCain called the overruns "disgraceful," "outrageous," and "a tragedy."[16]

Yet another example is the development of the Zumwalt, a new class of Navy destroyer stealth ship approved by Congress in 2006. The project, named after the late Navy Chief Admiral Elmo Zumwalt, originally called for building 32 vessels at the cost of $9.6 billion. Thirteen years later, the ship is still working through problems. The Navy now projects that developing and building three Zumwalts will cost the United States $23.5 billion, or almost $8 billion per ship, and they won't be combat-ready until late 2021.[17]

6. The Department of Defense's health insurance program is too rich. The Pentagon's health care budget is $51.4 billion for the 2020 fiscal year (which started October 1, 2019). That is up from $32.7 billion in 2014 and $16.3 billion in 2000.[18] The government provides almost free health care to all military retirees and their families for life, even if they are working in other jobs with health insurance. A soldier can join the Army at 18, retire at 38, and receive medical benefits for the rest of his or her life. Former Secretary of Defense Robert Gates tried to reform the Defense Department's health care program and failed. In addition, retirement ages in the military were set more than 100 years ago when the average life expectancy was younger than 60 years. Just like with Social Security, we need to change with the times, and the current health care policy for employees of the Defense Department cannot be sustained.

Afghanistan:
America's Trillion Dollar War

Cost of the Afghanistan conflict and troops deployed from 2001 to 2019

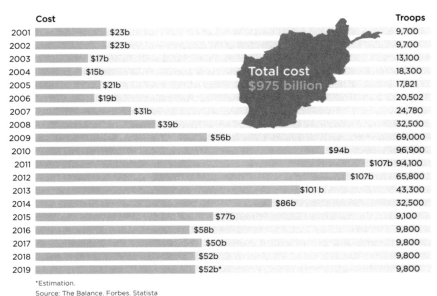

	Cost		Troops
2001	$23b		9,700
2002	$23b		9,700
2003	$17b		13,100
2004	$15b		18,300
2005	$21b		17,821
2006	$19b		20,502
2007	$31b		24,780
2008	$39b		32,500
2009	$56b		69,000
2010	$94b		96,900
2011		$107b	94,100
2012	$107b		65,800
2013	$101 b		43,300
2014	$86b		32,500
2015	$77b		9,100
2016	$58b		9,800
2017	$50b		9,800
2018	$52b		9,800
2019	$52b*		9,800

Total cost
$975 billion

*Estimation.
Source: The Balance. Forbes. Statista

7. The cost of the wars in Afghanistan and Iraq is an ongoing drain on our military budget. Most Americans have no idea how much money we are spending to continue to fight the wars in Iraq and Afghanistan. The total cost of the War on Terror is now estimated at $6.4 trillion, according to the Watson Institute at Brown University. Meanwhile, in February 2018, the Pentagon said the effort in Afghanistan was $45 billion each year.[19]

We are $23 trillion in debt, and in 2019 alone, our annual deficit with a booming economy was $984 billion. At the same time, our roads are falling apart, many of our children are attending substandard schools because they lack the funding, and yet we are spending $1 trillion per year for our nation's defense programs. We are making decisions like spending $8 billion per ship on a vessel that the Defense Department doesn't really want at a time when, for $5 billion, we could be providing Medicare for 1.5 million of our citizens who have no insurance. Or we could be doubling our funding for substance abuse programs to combat the opioid epidemic and the highest suicide rate we have seen in our country's history, or we could be reducing our nation's $23 trillion debt.

If I am elected president, I will work with our military to come up with a plan to reduce total Defense Department and related expenditures from $1 trillion to $850 billion in fiscal 2022 and $750 billion in fiscal 2023. This would be a reduction of $250 billion. I will host a meeting with the leadership team at the Defense Department along with key members of Congress to finalize a plan to meet those objectives. This plan will be called the *Defense Simplicity Act of 2021* and will be delivered to Congress within the first 90 days of my administration. I will request that Congress vote thumbs up or thumbs down on the entire package. It is my firm belief that we can reduce our defense spending by $250 billion, and we can do it with very little impact on the real defense needs of our country. We need to get rid of all the waste and make decisions that are in the best interest of the American people. Below are nine examples of opportunities to reduce spending that will be at the top of my list when I sit down with the leadership group of the Defense Department:

1. Maintain a single Department of Defense budget. I will eliminate the practice of balancing three different defense-related budgets and instead maintain a single budget to simplify the process and to allow American citizens transparency into how their government is spending money.

2. Review the Air Force budget, and cut the number of planes we have. The Air Force currently has over 5,000 jets and 87 different models of helicopters. In addition, the Army has nearly 4,000 aircraft, the Navy has 2,500, the Marines have more than 1,200, and the Coast Guard has 200. Add it all up, and we have 179 types of jets and helicopters in our arsenal of more than 13,000 aircraft.[20]

The F-35 and the B-1 planes cost billions to develop and were not deployed in any recent combat zones, including Iraq and Afghanistan. The United States has not been challenged by air for roughly 70 years. Southwest Airlines, one of the most successful and profitable commercial airlines in the United States, flies only Boeing 737 planes. We do not need 50 types of jets, and we cannot afford it. A reduction in the number of planes we deploy and a simplification in the models of planes we produce will save billions of dollars for the American taxpayer every year.

3. Review the Navy's budget and reduce expenditures. As an example of the size of the U.S. Navy compared to the rest of the world, we have 11 naval aircraft carriers; the rest of the world has only 9. The newest generation, the USS Gerald R. Ford, cost $13 billion, plus $4.7 billion for research and development. The project is two years behind schedule and at least 22 percent over budget.[21]

4. Reduce the size of the U.S. Marine Corps. As a nation, we have not conducted an amphibious landing since the Korean War in the early 1950s. The Marine Corps currently has more planes, ships, armored vehicles, and personnel in uniform—186,000 Marines—more than double the entire British Army.[22]

5. Reduce the size of the Army. We could save billions of dollars by cutting back the Army from around 478,000 to a force of 360,000. As warfare becomes more technologically oriented, we can make the tough decision to have fewer forces on the ground.

6. Reduce the size of our nuclear arsenal. The cost of maintaining the U.S. nuclear arsenal over the next 10 years has been estimated at $494 billion. We currently have more than 1,750 nuclear weapons deployed and another 4,400 stockpiled.[23] How many nuclear weapons do you want to pay for? Do we want to spend $494 billion over the next 10 years when we have so many other needs in our country? Reducing the size of our nuclear arsenal is a great opportunity to significantly reduce our defense budget.

7. Reduce overseas deployment of troops and bases. We currently have the same number of troops abroad as we did during the last decade of the Cold War. Reducing troops in Europe and Asia from 130,000 to 100,000 per year would save billions of dollars over the next 10 years.

8. Change the military retirement system. The current system allows military personnel to retire after 20 years of service, with inflation-adjusted benefits for the rest of their lives. We cannot afford to have someone join the military at 18, retire at 38, and receive a full pension and health care benefits for life. I will propose that we change the military retirement requirement from 20 years to 30 years for all people entering the military after March 31, 2021. At the same time, anyone in the military who is wounded in battle should receive the *best* medical care and have full benefits for life. With all of the money that we can save in the Department of Defense budget, a priority should be to take excellent care of those whose lives have been impacted by the battlefield.

9. I will withdraw ALL of our ground troops from Afghanistan and Iraq within two years. I will start to withdraw troops within six months of taking office. The War on Terror has now lasted 18 years and has spanned three presidencies. In 2001, Lawrence Lindsay, who was director of President George W. Bush's National Economic Council, projected that the War on Terror would cost $200 billion.[24] The current cost of the War on Terror, according to the Watson Institute at Brown University, is $6.4 trillion, along with more than 7,000 U.S. soldiers killed, at least 52,000 wounded Americans, and a total estimated at 800,000 deaths from the war violence in Iraq, Afghanistan, Syria, Yemen and Pakistan.[25] After 18 years, it is time to take our combat troops out of Afghanistan and Iraq, and if we need to continue to send a message, do it from the air. Annual cost savings achieved by getting out of Afghanistan and Iraq would be at least $50 billion per year, according to my estimate.

In 1953, President Eisenhower gave one of the most historic of all presidential farewell addresses. What did Eisenhower, a lifelong military man, talk about? The growing military-industrial complex and what he feared could happen in the future. He stated this:

A vital element in keeping the peace is our military establishment. Our arms must be mighty, ready for instant action, so that no potential aggressor may be tempted to risk his own destruction. Our military organization today bears little relation to that known by any of my predecessors in peacetime, or, indeed, by the fighting men of World War II or Korea.

Until the latest of our world conflicts, the United States had no armaments industry. American makers of plowshares could, with time and as required, make swords as well. But we can no longer risk emergency improvisation of national defense; we have been compelled to create a permanent armaments industry of vast proportions. Added to this, three and a half million men and women are directly engaged in the defense establishment. We annually spend on military security more than the net income of all United States corporations.

This conjunction of an immense military establishment and a large arms industry is new in the American experience. The total influence—economic, political, and even spiritual—is felt in every city, every state, every office of the federal government. We recognize the imperative need for this development. Yet, we must not fail to comprehend its grave implications. Our toil, resources, and livelihood are all involved; so is the very structure of our society.

In the councils of government, we must guard against the acquisition of unwarranted influence, whether sought or unsought, by the military-industrial complex. The potential for the disastrous rise of misplaced power exists and will persist.

We must never let the weight of this combination endanger our liberties or democratic processes. We should take nothing for granted. Only an alert and knowledgeable citizenry can compel the proper meshing of the huge industrial and military machinery of defense with our peaceful methods and goals, so that security and liberty may prosper together.[26]

In retrospect, everything that Eisenhower feared has come to fruition. We have a huge military-industrial establishment that spends $1 trillion per year (more than the next eight nations combined). The military-industrial complex spends roughly $100 million a year to lobby Congress to keep spending billions of dollars more on the military than we need. We must start making decisions that are in the best interests of the citizens of the United States, not in the best interests of the military-industrial complex. Just like every business or any individual family, we need to make choices, and we need to continuously evaluate our spending. The $250 billion saved could go toward paying down our debt or funding other programs that the country desperately needs.

If you had a choice, would you spend $250 billion on upgrading our nuclear arms program or $250 billion on upgrading our transportation system? Or $250 billion on cutting childhood poverty in half? Or $250 billion on reducing our debt so that our children don't have to deal with it? To maximize the potential of our nation, we are going to need everyone to make sacrifices, including the military. ✔

9

Return to a Responsible Foreign Policy

"Words can destroy. What we call each other, ultimately becomes what we think of each other, and it matters."

—Jeane Kirkpatrick, the first woman to serve as
U.S. ambassador to the United Nations, 1981–1985[1]

At the start of the 21st century, the mission statement of the State Department read: "To advance freedom for the benefit of the American people and the international community by helping to build and sustain a more democratic, secure, and prosperous world composed of well-governed states that respond to the needs of their people, reduce widespread poverty, and act responsibly within the international system."[2]

There has been more change in America's foreign policy in the first three years of the Trump administration than there was in the previous 50 years. The changes have been profound:

Roosevelt/Reagan policy:	Trump policy:
Optimism	"The world is an angry place."
Tearing walls down	Building walls
Welcoming immigrants	Immigrants are not welcome
Treating allies with respect	Treating allies like adversaries
Everyone can win	America first
America as the global leader	American isolationism: "Let's take care of ourselves."

Why should foreign policy matter to you?

1. As time goes by, the world is getting smaller. Seventy years ago, it took 30 days to travel from New York City to Germany. Today, it takes eight hours. The computer, the internet, and the smartphone have all revolutionized the way the world communicates and conducts global business. As the world gets smaller, our neighbors have a greater impact on us. We either become closer friends or more bitter enemies. Friendship has benefits: trade partners are formed, new markets are opened, peace can be expanded. An effective foreign policy in an age where the world is getting smaller can make a big difference to every American. A good foreign policy can make the difference between war and peace. When countries cooperate, they can also work together to help curb the spread of virulent diseases —such as COVID-19—and maybe even collaborate to find a cure.

2. The global economy. As the world becomes smaller, trade between nations increases. In 2018, 12.2 percent of the goods and services produced in the U.S. were sold in other countries.[3] Worldwide, 59.4 percent of the global economy depends on sales that companies make to consumers and businesses in other countries, according to the World Bank.[4] The bottom line is our economy is very dependent on business involving other nations. That reliance on foreign customers has soared in recent years. In 1960, U.S. companies reported $25.9 billion in global trade;[5] today, that number is $2.5 trillion, 100 times the 1960 level.[6]

The better relationships we have around the world, the more markets we can open, and the more people will be interested in investing in the United States.

An increase in global trade means more better-paying jobs for Americans, and it also means a higher standard of living as Americans have access to less expensive goods. We are exporting products like GE medical equipment and Boeing airliners, and we import products like inexpensive clothing (a pair of Rustler blue jeans at Walmart sells for $12.97) and shoes so Americans can buy more with their

Exports of Goods and Services

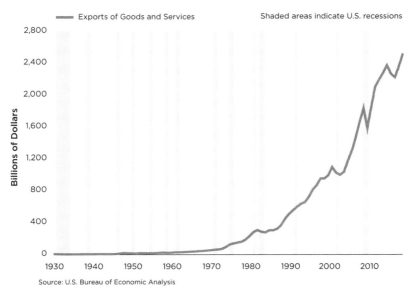

Source: U.S. Bureau of Economic Analysis

dollars. Increased global trade leads to greater opportunities for American workers and American companies. Increased trade and mutually beneficial commerce lead to stronger relationships that keep the peace.

3. Security. It is said that in the history of the world, 90 percent of wars have been started because of miscommunication. Foreign policy helps to keep the world at peace. Peace means the free flow of goods, the free flow of information, and it also means that our sons and daughters are not fighting wars. David Brooks wrote the following about foreign policy in an editorial in *The New York Times*:[7]

> Most of human history has been marked by war. Between 1500 and 1945, scarcely a year went by without some great power fighting another great power. Then, in 1945 that stopped. The number of battlefield deaths has plummeted to the lowest levels in history. The world has experienced the greatest reduction in poverty in history, as well as the greatest spread of democracy and freedom. Why did this happen? Mostly it was because the United States decided to lead a community of nations to create a democratic world order: That order consisted of institutions like NATO, the U.N., and the World Bank. But it was also enforced by the pervasive presence of American power—military, economic and cultural power as well as the magnetic power of the democratic idea, which inspired dissidents worldwide.... But the U.S. having been dragged into two world wars, leaders from Truman through Obama felt they had no choice but to widen America's circle of concern across the whole world. This was abnormal. As Robert Kagan writes in *The Jungle Grows Back*, "Very few nations in history have ever felt a responsibility for anything but themselves."

An effective American foreign policy has a huge impact on every American citizen. It also has a massive impact on every citizen around the globe. We should take great pride in the stability our foreign policy has brought to the world since the end of World War II, and we should be scared stiff about the "America first" foreign policy of the Trump administration where the world is angry, where there are winners and losers, and where we side more and more with dictators and watch as some historic alliances hit their low points.

4. United States foreign policy has made a positive impact on the world. Much of the world depends on us! We have a long, proud tradition of playing a leadership role in keeping the peace around the globe. In his final letter to America, Senator John McCain summed up America's role in the world with these words: "We are citizens of the world's greatest republic, a nation of ideals, not blood and soil. We are blessed and are a blessing to humanity when we uphold and advance those ideals at home and in the world. We have helped liberate more people from tyranny and poverty than ever before in history. We have acquired great wealth and power in the process."[8]

5. Climate change. One of the greatest challenges of our time is climate change. If we fail to reverse what 97 percent of scientists believe is human-caused climate change, it will have a massive impact on our environment, our economy, and our lives. We will have a disaster on our hands. The best way to solve the global environmental crisis is to work with other like-minded countries. We are all responsible for the resources we share on our planet, and an effective foreign policy can help to combat climate change. We need friends to get things done in the world.

6. A strong democracy. The cornerstone of our government is our democracy—one person, one vote. In 2016, according to the FBI, the CIA, and the Justice Department, the Russians interfered in our elections.[9] With advancements in technology, more of our global adversaries will attempt to influence our elections. In the future, a strong foreign policy is key to ensuring a strong, stable democracy within the United States.

7. Foreign policy failures are costly. The U.S. wars in Iraq and Afghanistan have cost the American taxpayer more than $5.9 trillion since 9/11.[10] While foreign policy is not going to prevent all military action, great cooperation among like-minded nations over the years has prevented many wars. It was foreign policy that prevented the Cuban Missile Crisis from becoming a global disaster.

If I am elected president, you can expect the following from me when it comes to foreign policy:

1. Global leadership. I will return the United States to an active foreign policy and provide global leadership. My administration will treat our friends with the respect they deserve, and we will have an optimistic view of the future. Some people want us to return to a globe where nationalism beats internationalism, the same philosophy that brought about two world wars. I reject that thinking, and I will work with like-minded leaders around the world to create a more secure, prosperous, and democratic world.

James Mattis, President Donald Trump's first Secretary of Defense, said in his new book, "To preserve our leadership role, we needed to get our own country's act together first, especially if we were to help others. An oft-spoken admonition in the Marines is this: When you're going to a gunfight, bring all your friends with guns. Having fought many times in coalitions, I believe that we need every ally we can bring to the fight. From imaginative military solutions to their country's vote in the U.N., the more allies the better. I have never been on a crowded battlefield, and there is always room for those who want to be there alongside us."[11]

I completely agree with Secretary Mattis. Having friends around the world is a good thing, and if I am elected, my administration will work to foster great relationships across the globe.

2. I will put the best team on the field. I will make sure that we have an exceptional Secretary of State and that we fill the State Department with a team of people who have a proven track record of success.

3. I will expand the Peace Corps budget from $410.5 million to $10.4 billion.[12] I will propose to Congress that we take $10 billion of the $250 billion that we will save in the Defense Department and create an expanded Peace Corps 2.0. *New York Times* columnist Thomas Friedman explained in one of his columns that "if the Army, Navy, Air Force, Coast Guard, and Marine Corps constitute our 'defense,' the Peace Corps would be our 'offense.' Its primary task would be to work at the village and neighborhood levels to help create economic opportunity and improve governance, helping more people to live decently in their home countries and not feel forced to move to other nations."[13] As an example, Friedman wrote about the Arab awakening in May 2012: "During that time, the United States made two financial commitments to the Arab world that each began with the numbers 1 and 3. It gave Egypt's military $1.3 billion worth of tanks and fighter jets, and it gave Lebanese public school students a $13.5 million merit-based college scholarship program that is currently putting 117 Lebanese kids through local American-style colleges that promote tolerance, gender and social equality.... The $13.5 million in full scholarships has already bought America so much more friendship and stability than the $1.3 billion in tanks and fighter jets ever will.... Jumana Jbar, an English teacher in an Amman public school, summed it up better than I ever could: One is 'for making people,' she said, 'and the other is for killing people.'"[14]

As a nation, if we want different results, we need to try different things. Elevating the Peace Corps and spending part of our defense savings on building hope around the world would be a new approach and a worthy investment. If the Peace Corps 2.0 approach works, it could have a major impact on United States foreign policy for the next 50 years. If it fails, I will shut it down after a two-year trial period.

4. American troops on the ground as a last resort. I would put troops on the ground as a last resort to any international problem. We learned in Vietnam and Iraq and Afghanistan that we could not use our massive military might to solve all problems. We cannot transplant our political culture. We have spent $5.9 trillion since 9/11 fighting wars, and in my administration, we will only put boots on the ground as a last resort. At the same time, if we cannot solve a crisis through diplomacy, and if force is necessary, I am a strong believer in the Powell Doctrine of overwhelming force. We have massive military power, and if, as a last resort, it needs to be used, I will make sure we have a clear objective, and I will use overwhelming force to accomplish that objective.

In the 243 years we have existed as a country, we have made some mistakes, but we have done more to liberate people from tyranny and poverty than any country in history. We can take great pride in the fact that America has made the world a better place. As our world becomes smaller, as technology increases the speed of our world, and as we face big issues like climate change and nuclear sanity, the future of the world depends on American leadership. The world is not a zero-sum game. For every winner, there does not need to be a loser. For every growing economy, there does not need to be a shrinking one. Our security and our prosperity have the best chance when other countries are also successful.

If I am elected president, I will use the foreign policy of the United States to build positive relationships around the world to make the world more secure and more prosperous. When America helps to create a global environment where countries are more secure and more prosperous, hundreds of millions of lives can be positively impacted. That impact, in turn, can have a positive effect on America. ◆

10

Reduce Gun Deaths in America

"At the end of the day, the students at my school felt one shared experience—our politicians abandoned us by failing to keep guns out of schools."

—Cameron Kasky, 17-year old student who survived the mass shooting at Marjory Stoneman Douglas High School in Parkland, Florida in 2018[1]

We have a problem with gun violence in America.

Nearly 40,000 people—39,773 to be precise—died from gunshot wounds in 2017, the Centers for Disease Control and Prevention says. That includes homicides, suicides—which account for about six of every 10 gun deaths in the United States—as well as unintentional shootings and law enforcement-related incidents.[2]

It is the highest gun mortality rate in the U.S. in 50 years, and it translates into 12 gun deaths per 100,000 people, according to a Pew

Center Report in August 2019.[3] By comparison, Australia reported one gun death per 100,000 population.[4] That means you are 12 times more likely to be shot and killed in the United States than you are in Australia. How about Japan? Only 0.04 of every 100,000 people were gun death victims there in 2017, the Institute for Health Metrics and Evaluation says.[5] Your chances of being shot and killed in the United States are 300 times more likely than they are in Japan.

Why is the United States so much more violent than any other civilized country in the world? Why are your chances of being shot so much higher in the United States than any other civilized nation in the world? The answer is that we lack simple gun control laws. We have debated the issue of gun control for the last 55 years with no progress. It is my opinion, based on the following facts, that we need to change the gun laws in the United States:

1. More than 14,500 people were murdered by gunfire in the United States in 2017; another 24,000 people used guns to take their own lives. As many as 100,000 more are wounded in gun incidents in the U.S. every year, according to the nonprofit organization Everytown for Gun Safety.[6] The number of people who die each year from gunfire in our country is well over 10 times the number of people who died at Pearl Harbor (2,403) or lost their lives on 9/11 (2,977). These two events, though tragic, galvanized the national will of the vast majority of Americans. The country acted, declaring war against its attackers—Japan, in the first case, and terrorists in the aftermath of 9/11. There has not been another single, defining, national event as catastrophic as Pearl Harbor or 9/11. Yet every year, thousands of Americans are killed, take their own lives, or are wounded as a result of gun violence.

Over 10 years, the U.S. recorded around 300,000 gun-related deaths (about 60 percent of them were suicides) and as many as one million

The U.S. Gun Homicide Rate is 25 Times that of Other High-Income Countries

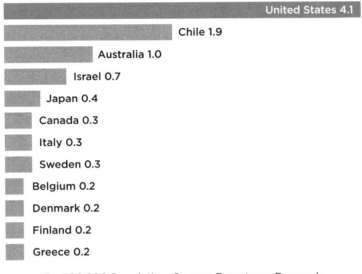

United States 4.1
Chile 1.9
Australia 1.0
Israel 0.7
Japan 0.4
Canada 0.3
Italy 0.3
Sweden 0.3
Belgium 0.2
Denmark 0.2
Finland 0.2
Greece 0.2

Per 100,000 Population. Source: Everytown Research.
https://everytownresearch.org/gun-violence-america/

firearms-related injuries, based on figures from the Centers for Disease Control and nonprofit groups such as the Giffords Law Center to Prevent Gun Violence.[7] As a nation, we should be appalled and embarrassed by these numbers. In the United States, 12 people lose their lives from gunshots for every 100,000 residents. Our friends in Canada have two gun deaths per 100,000, while in Australia, Germany, and Spain, only one or fewer per 100,000 population are killed by guns, the Pew study shows.[8]

Why is Australia so low? I will give you two guesses: (A) They have the same gun laws as the United States but they have really nice people; or (B) They had a big gun problem in Australia and the government changed the laws in 1996 to ban all automatic and semi-automatic weapons. If you picked B, you are the winner! The sad truth is that the United States is one of the most violent countries in the world, and we have done nothing to solve the problem.[9]

2. Gun violence is costing the U.S. economy more than $229 billion per year.[10] Just think about the health care costs of taking care of the 100,000 people who are shot every year but survive; productivity lost from those who cannot work; jail costs for those who ruin lives by using firearms; police costs, etc. Just ask any mayor of Big City, U.S.A. what would happen to their police budgets if the gun control laws in this country were the same as any other civilized country in the world. They would tell you their budgets could be significantly less than what they currently are. I went to a high school graduation recently, and lurking in the background were two sheriff's cars and an ambulance. At a high school graduation? Who is paying

Firearms Are the Second Leading Cause of Death for American Children and Teens

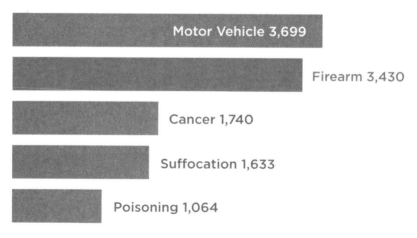

Motor Vehicle 3,699

Firearm 3,430

Cancer 1,740

Suffocation 1,633

Poisoning 1,064

Source: COC, Fatal Injury Reports, 2017

the cost to have these resources at a high school graduation in case there is a shooting? As a nation that is $23 trillion in debt and spends almost twice as much on health care as any other country, we simply cannot afford the cost of having nearly 140,000 of our fellow citizens shot every year.

3. It is time. Just take a look at presidential history and the gun. Several presidential candidates and presidents have been victims of gunfire. In the last 120 years alone, Theodore Roosevelt was shot during the 1912 election; Franklin Roosevelt was shot at in Miami after he won the presidency in 1933; an assassination attempt was made on Harry Truman in 1950, resulting in the death of a White House policeman; John F. Kennedy was assassinated in 1963; his brother, Robert Kennedy, was shot and killed in the 1968 presidential campaign; George Wallace was shot and ended up in a wheelchair in the 1972 campaign; Gerald Ford survived two assassination attempts in 1975; and Ronald Reagan was shot only three months into his presidency in 1981.

We have witnessed massacres at Columbine High School in Littleton, Colorado, where 14 kids and a teacher died; at Sandy Hook Elementary School in Newtown, Connecticut, which resulted in the deaths of 20 children and six educators; at Marjory Stoneman Douglas High School in Parkland, Florida, where 14 high school students and three staff members were murdered. In 2018, there were 24 school shootings.

We have seen Representative Gabrielle Giffords shot in the head and suffer permanent disability,[11] and in 2015, we saw a year of gun violence in America that is hard to believe. According to *The Washington Post*, in the first 274 days of 2015, there were 294 mass shootings, defined as when four or more people are shot.[12] Nine people were shot dead in a church in Charleston, South Carolina; 14 people were killed and

22 injured in a mass shooting in San Bernardino, California; 49 died in a nightclub shooting in Orlando, Florida.

More recently, in October 2017, a gunman firing from a 32nd-floor hotel room in Las Vegas killed 58 innocent victims at an outdoor music festival and injured another 500. In October 2018, 11 people were killed at a synagogue in Pittsburgh; and in November 2018,

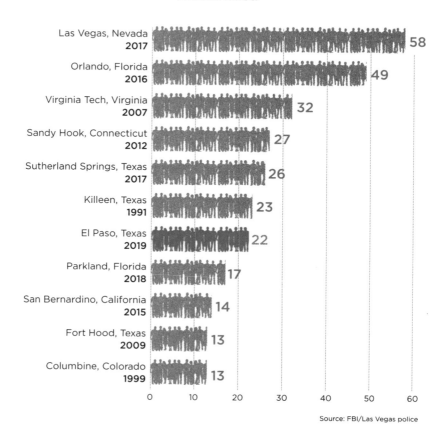

Worst Mass Shootings in the U.S. since 1991

Victims killed

Location	Victims killed
Las Vegas, Nevada 2017	58
Orlando, Florida 2016	49
Virginia Tech, Virginia 2007	32
Sandy Hook, Connecticut 2012	27
Sutherland Springs, Texas 2017	26
Killeen, Texas 1991	23
El Paso, Texas 2019	22
Parkland, Florida 2018	17
San Bernardino, California 2015	14
Fort Hood, Texas 2009	13
Columbine, Colorado 1999	13

Source: FBI/Las Vegas police

13 people died in a shooting incident at the Borderline Bar and Grill in Thousand Oaks, California.

During the first 237 days of 2019, there were 290 mass shootings reported nationwide.[13] They included one horrifying weekend in early August when a gunman opened fire at a Walmart packed with shoppers in El Paso, Texas, leaving 22 people dead and 24 injured. Then, less than 24 hours later, nine people were shot to death and 27 wounded outside a bar in Dayton, Ohio. Police shot and killed that suspect.

The August 3 and 4 incidents came one week after a mass shooting at the Gilroy, California, Garlic Festival, where 16 people were injured, and four lost their lives, including the gunman.

And then, August ended with two West Texas towns ripped by tragedy as a man, just fired from his trucking job, fired at motorists and law enforcement officers as he drove, leaving 25 people wounded and seven dead between Midland and Odessa.

What have we done as a nation to fix this problem? Nothing. Great nations deal with reality, and the reality of the situation is that we need to do something. Ezra Klein, writing for *The Washington Post*, put it best:

> If roads were collapsing all across the United States, killing dozens of drivers, we would surely see that as a moment to talk about what we could do to keep the roads from collapsing. If terrorists were detonating bombs in port after port, you can be sure Congress would be working to upgrade the nation's security measures. If a plague were ripping through communities, public health officials would be working feverishly to contain it.

Only with gun violence do we respond to repeated tragedies by saying that mourning is acceptable but discussing how to prevent more tragedies is not.... Talking about how to stop mass shootings in the aftermath of a string of mass shootings isn't "too soon." It's much too late.[14]

4. The world has changed since the Second Amendment of the Constitution was ratified in 1791. The Second Amendment of the Constitution does not guarantee the right of citizens to walk around our streets with assault rifles.

The Second Amendment states the following: "A well-regulated militia, being necessary to the security of a free state, the right of the people to keep and bear arms, shall not be infringed." Do we really think our Founding Fathers would support semi-automatic rifles that disperse 20 bullets in as many seconds? Their intent was the protection of the nation at a time when there were relatively few people in the military, and citizens had to be prepared. Think of Paul Revere riding his horse to warn the citizens that "The British are coming!" At that point in time, our government needed citizens like Paul Revere to be armed in order to protect the country.

Nearly one million women alive today have been shot or shot at by an intimate partner

Source: Sorenson SB, Schut RA. Nonfatal gun use in intimate partner violence: A systematic review of the literature. *Trauma Violence Abuse*, 2016

Today, we have the Army, the Air Force, the Navy, the Marines, and the Coast Guard. In addition, we have police in every city across our country. We do not need citizens to be armed with semi-automatic weapons to protect our country.

Second Amendment supporters frequently quote the Constitution as stating that "the right of the people to keep and bear arms shall not be infringed." They forget to mention the 13 words that precede that phrase, in the same sentence: "A well-regulated militia, being necessary to the security of a free state ... the right of the people to keep and bear arms shall not be infringed." Chief Justice Warren Burger, a conservative appointed by a Republican president, said in a 1991 PBS interview that the Second Amendment "has been the subject of one of the greatest pieces of fraud, I repeat the word fraud, on the American public by special interest groups that I have ever seen in my lifetime."[15]

5. The majority of Americans support common-sense measures to prevent gun violence. Three separate polls in 2019 showed that 89 percent of Americans support expanding background checks on gun purchases.[16] Yet the gun lobby protects the views of the 11 percent who disagree. Is our government elected to represent the 89 percent majority or the 11 percent minority? The National Rifle Association has convinced its members that any kind of gun control is the same as having your guns taken away.

If I am elected your president, I will move to end gun violence in America by proposing the *Gabby Giffords Violence Reduction Act of 2021*. The simple solutions in this proposed legislation are as follows:

emptied 33 rounds
in less than 30 seconds

1. Ban all assault rifles and extended magazines. The Glock 19 semi-automatic pistol that was used in Representative Gabby Giffords' shooting emptied 33 rounds in less than 30 seconds.[17]

These were the guns used in some of the other recent mass shootings:

Odessa: AR-15 style rifle[18]

Dayton: AR-15 style pistol with a 100-round magazine[19]

El Paso: AK-47 style rifle[20]

Gilroy: WASR-10 semi-automatic rifle, a variant of the AK-47[21]

Thousand Oaks: Glock 21 .45-caliber semi-automatic pistol with an extended magazine[22]

Pittsburgh: Colt AR-15 rifle and three Glock .357 handguns[23]

Las Vegas: 23 firearms were found, including at least a dozen semi-automatic rifles with bump stocks[24]

In addition to banning all assault rifles, the *Gabby Giffords Violence Reduction Act* will get all assault rifles off the streets by launching a program to buy back all of these weapons. People who currently own assault weapons will be paid the current value or the price for which they purchased the gun, whichever is higher. In 1996, Australia banned assault rifles and extended clips, and the homicide rate plummeted 59 percent over the next decade.[25]

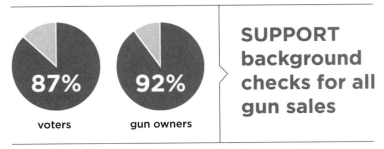

About 20 percent of purchased guns require no background check.

87% voters

92% gun owners

SUPPORT background checks for all gun sales

2. Impose a universal background check on 100 percent of guns purchased and set up a nationwide database of gun owners. A large number of Americans think federal laws require a background check for every gun purchase and that the laws ban high-capacity magazines, but that is incorrect! An estimated 22 percent of gun purchases are made without a background check.[26] Polls show 90 percent of Americans[27] think background checks should also be required for people who buy guns in private transactions or at gun shows. Let's give the people what they want and require that all gun owners have a background check.

The shooter in Odessa, Texas, determined in court to be mentally unfit to own a gun, was stopped from purchasing a weapon from a licensed gun dealer in 2014, law enforcement officers told the Associated Press. But thanks to a loophole in the law, he bought his rifle through a private sale, not covered by federal background check requirements.[28]

Currently in America, any time a cop wants to connect a gun to its owner, the request ends up at the National Tracing Center in Martinsburg, West Virginia. On any given day, agents are running about 1,500 traces on a shoestring budget, sorting through boxes of paper records, thanks to a law the NRA worked to get Congress to pass in 1986, preventing a simple, searchable database of gun owners from being established.[29]

3. Require mandatory gun licenses for gun owners. Guns should be treated the same as cars. Why do you need to get a license in order to drive and get a car registered? Because driving a car is a big responsibility, and if you misuse the car, you can cause serious damage, not only to yourself but to others. Operating a gun is as dangerous as operating a car, if not more so. People should have to get a license to have a gun. It is in everyone's interest to make sure that everyone who has a gun is capable of safe gun ownership. Right now, you can go to a gun show and buy a gun and never have to get it registered. That would be like having to get a registration for a new car but not for a used one. The NRA has convinced its members that it is a bad thing to require guns to be registered. It is not a bad thing; it is a common-sense practice that would benefit all Americans, whether you own a gun or not.

4. Repeal the Protection of Lawful Commerce in Arms Act. This law bans lawsuits against gun manufacturers and sellers for the harm that they cause and immunizes the gun industry from responsibility for the thousands of gun deaths every year.

In the 2017 Las Vegas shooting, where 58 people were massacred and hundreds more injured, the hotel is being sued, the concert organizers are being sued, but the Protection of Lawful Commerce in Arms Act, supported by the NRA, has shielded the gun industry from lawsuits—until recently. Lawyers for the parents of one victim filed suit last summer against eight manufacturers of AR-15-style guns, saying the way they are designed makes it easy to modify them so they become automatic rifles.[30]

If I am elected president, I will provide the leadership to make sure that eliminating gun violence is at the top of my administration's agenda, and I will make it a cause to ensure that the days of our nation's leaders failing to provide safe schools and safe public places come to an end. American citizens should not live in fear when they go out in public, and they should not have to worry when they send their kids off to school in the morning if they will see them at the end of the day.

We do so many amazing things as a country, but we need to face the fact that we are one of the most violent countries in the world. The violence that the NRA and our gun laws allow to occur, year after year, is an embarrassment to our great nation. Susan Orfanos, whose son was killed in the Thousand Oaks shooting after surviving the Las Vegas massacre, said in a TV interview that she doesn't want prayers. "I don't want thoughts, I want gun control, and I hope to God nobody sends me any more prayers," Orfanos said.

If I am elected president, I will send to Congress the *Gabby Giffords Violence Reduction Act of 2021* during my first month in office. No prayers, no thoughts—just simple, clear, bold legislation so we can regulate guns the same way we regulate cars and put an end to the madness.

We can save the nation billions of dollars and, most importantly, we can save tens of thousands of lives every single year and prevent misery for so many families affected by gun violence across America. ✔

11

Fix the Legal System

"Equal justice under the law is not merely a caption on the facade of the Supreme Court building. It is perhaps the most inspiring ideal in our society."

—Former U.S. Supreme Court Justice Lewis F. Powell, Jr.[1]

The American legal system is broken. While there are a lot of good lawyers in America who do some exceptional work, no one comes to America to study our legal system. Lawyers in America are feasting on a defective system, and because they donate significant sums of money to political candidates, they keep the system intact. In fact, as time goes on, the system gets worse. The worse the system is, the more the legal profession benefits. Anyone can be sued for anything, no matter how ridiculous. In addition to the way our laws are administered, we now have 2.3 million of our fellow citizens in jail or prison.[2]

The company I work for was sued for patent infringement on a bicycle design. We actually had a real example of the prototype we had independently developed and a mountain of other evidence that we did not infringe. We won the case, but only after spending $3 million in legal fees. Or how about the Trek retailer who held a special event for women? He was sued by a male consumer for discrimination because the guy was not invited to the event. The retailer settled the case for $17,000 because his lawyer told him that if he fought it, he could lose more than $100,000. Finally, in a small, Southern California community, a neighborhood group put in speed bumps to slow down traffic and improve safety. A teenager riding a motorized scooter over the speed limit hit a speed bump and crashed. The parents sued the neighborhood association for more than $1 million, and the neighbors settled for $250,000 on the advice of their lawyers.

These are just three stories out of millions more about how our legal system lacks common sense, is overly bureaucratic, and never gets updated or improved. It just gets worse with time.

If I am elected president, I will propose that we overhaul our legal system so we can significantly increase fairness, cut our prison population in half, increase the speed of our justice system, and create a better business environment, which will create more jobs.

What evidence exists to prove that our legal system needs a complete overhaul?

1. We have too many lawyers. Our country has too many lawyers, and they have created the most litigious society in history. Warren Burger, former chief justice of the U.S. Supreme Court, predicted 40 years ago that America was turning into "a society overrun by hordes of lawyers, hungry as locusts."[3] According to the *Boston Globe*, "With 1.3 million lawyers ... the United States is choking on litigation, regulation, and disputation."[4] How do we fare compared to other countries in the number of lawyers per capita?

The U.S. has 391 lawyers for every 100,000 people compared to the United Kingdom with 251 lawyers per 100,000 and Canada with 26 lawyers per 100,000, according to a 2010 study at Harvard University. It's probably not surprising then to learn that in the U.S., 5,806 lawsuits are filed per 100,000 people, while in the U.K., the number is 3,681 and in Canada, 1,450, the study shows.[5]

2. Even our government is inundated with lawyers. In the current 116th Congress, 145 House members and 47 senators are lawyers, according to the Congressional Research Service.[6]

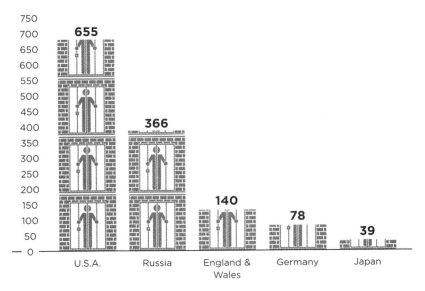

Prisoners per 100,000

Source: World Prison Brief, Institute for Crime & Justice Policy Research.
Reported in 2019 in *US News & World Report*

3. We have more prisoners than any country in the world. The numbers don't lie. As reported by Adam Liptak, Supreme Court correspondent for *The New York Times*, although less than 5 percent of the world's population lives in the United States, our country's prisoners amount to nearly 25 percent of the world's prison population.[7] The United States has 2.3 million people locked behind bars. This equates to 655 people in jail or prison for every 100,000. Meanwhile, the U.K. has 140 prisoners per 100,000; Germany has 77 per 100,000; and Japan has 39 per 100,000.[8] Either these countries are doing something right that we are missing, or there are a lot of people roaming their streets who should be locked up. My guess is that we have way too many people behind bars.

4. We are spending a lot of money locking people up. According to a 2014 report by the Hamilton Project, a part of the Brookings Institution, the total cost of America's prison system in 2010 was $80 billion.[9] If the total number of inmates in the United States is approximately 2.3 million, that means the average cost of locking someone up in the United States was approximately $35,000 per year.[10]

If I am elected president, within the first 30 days of my administration, I will send to the Congress the *Warren Burger Judicial Reform Act of 2021*. This proposal will make these two modifications to our judicial system:

1. Require losers of litigation to pay attorney fees and litigation costs of the winner. In the United States, we have a massive number of lawsuits because people can sue anyone for anything with no personal risk. Why so many lawsuits? Because lawyers encourage people to file lawsuits by not charging them any money unless they win. And if they win, they take a percentage of the winnings. Neither the person filing the lawsuit nor the lawyer taking the case has any real risk. By making one simple change and adopting the English Rule, where the losing party would pay the legal fees *and* the costs of the prevailing party, we would reduce lawsuits in this country by 50 percent to 75 percent.

Every civilized democracy operates with the English Rule for a reason. Many countries around the world have copied parts of our government; no country has followed our process for suing people. None. If we adopt the English Rule in the United States, lawyers would not want to take on cases that they did not think they could win. The result would be a significant reduction in the number of court cases in our system, the cases in the system would be dealt with much faster, and most importantly, companies would not have to suffer through frivolous lawsuits that are costing this country billions of dollars. The result would be a significantly better business climate in the United States, which would create hundreds of thousands or millions of new jobs.

2. My administration will set the goal of reducing the prison population in the United States by 50 percent by the end of 2024. We cannot spend $80 billion a year locking up 655 people per 100,000 while the rest of the Western world averages fewer than 150 people per 100,000 in prison, according to the World Prison Brief, an online database that uses United Nations statistics.[11]

This will be accomplished by:

- **Reducing sentences for nonviolent crimes, especially drug users.** There are almost 450,000 nonviolent drug users in our federal, state, and local prison systems today compared to 40,000 in 1980.[12]

Non-Violent Drug Users in Prison

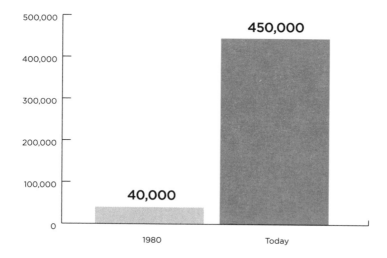

- **Change the bail system in the United States.** Many of our citizens can't pay bail, so they sit in jail. For example, two people are accused of the same crime. One has money and the other doesn't. The one with money hires a good lawyer and gets out on bail the same day. The second one sits in jail for up to six months— or longer—and gets a court-appointed attorney. The bail business is extremely lucrative, producing $2 billion of profits per year.[13] I will propose that we overhaul the bail system so everyone receives the same treatment regardless of their economic status.

- **Allow federal and state judges to use their discretion during the sentencing process.** Judges are professionals, and they know their business better than legislators. Two Supreme Court justices have expressed disapproval of mandatory sentences. Former Chief Justice William Rehnquist has said that mandatory sentences are "a good example of the law of unintended consequences."[14]

Former Justice Anthony Kennedy said, "I think I'm in agreement with most judges in the federal system that mandatory minimums are an imprudent, unwise, and often unjust mechanism for sentencing."[15]

There is a great essay written by Denver District Court Judge Morris Hoffman who in 1995 sentenced a teenage armed robber to 146 years in prison. In an article published in *The Wall Street Journal*, he wrote about the injustice of extreme sentences.

I think that Judge Hoffman's story is a very important one for Americans to understand:

In 1995, I sentenced a teenage armed robber to 146 years in prison. Believe it or not, that was just a little over the mandatory minimum sentence. With good time and "early" release on parole, he could be out as soon as 2065, having served a little less than 70 years. He'll be almost 90. The teenager's crime was horrible. He robbed a small restaurant at gunpoint, ordered the patrons onto the floor and ended up having a shootout with one customer who happened to have a gun. Miraculously, the only person injured was the robber, who was shot in the foot.

Today, we lead the Western world in average length of prison sentences, at 63 months. According to the Justice Policy Institute, Canada's average is four months, Finland's 10, Germany's 12, and rugged, individualistic Australia's average prison term is 36 months.

These numbers are even more striking considering that the modern prison is an American invention and the average sentence started out at a few months, not years. The Quakers invented prisons in the late 1700s as a more humane alternative to death or banishment, then the punishment for all serious crimes. But the penitentiary wasn't intended to be a criminal warehouse. Criminals were expected to work, pray and think about their crimes—to be penitent about them in a kind of moral rehabilitation. A 1785 New York statute was typical: It limited all non-homicide prison sentences to six months. French diplomat and historian Alexis de Tocqueville, whose visits to America began with a tour of U.S. prisons in 1831, wrote, "In no country is criminal justice administered with more mildness than in the United States." But over the next 150 years, America went from mildest punisher to harshest.

We have a duty to punish wrongdoers, but that duty comes with the obligation not to punish criminals more than they deserve. Much of our criminal justice system has lost that moral grounding, and our use of prisons has become extreme. It won't be easy. No one gets elected by calling for shorter prison sentences. But as a policy matter, there is simply no evidence that, say, a 70-year sentence for aggravated robbery does more than a 30-year sentence to deter other potential robbers. Moreover, violent crime rates decrease rapidly as criminals age out of their 20s. Releasing a middle-aged prisoner earlier does pose more risk, of course, than keeping him behind bars, but that marginal danger will be very small indeed when we are comparing 30-year and 70-year sentences.[16]

I agree with Judge Hoffman that "no one gets elected by calling for shorter prison sentences." And yet, I am calling for shorter prison terms. I am also calling for changing the way we administer bail, and I am calling for adopting the English Rule of Law. Our legal system is not working, and I believe it needs massive change.

If I am elected president, I will propose more change to our legal system than any president has proposed in the past 100 years. Enacting these proposals would save taxpayers over $30 billion a year and will trigger a significant increase in the economy because businesses will not have to worry about defending themselves against frivolous lawsuits. Most importantly, enacting these proposals would take 1.2 million nonviolent Americans out of prison and give them a chance to be productive, taxpaying citizens. It is said that no one ever got elected in America by campaigning for shorter prison sentences. I hope to be the first! ✓

12

Embrace the Immigration Advantage

"I am a beneficiary of the American
people's generosity, and I hope we can have
comprehensive immigration legislation that
allows this country to continue to be enriched
by those who were not born here."

—Madeleine Albright, the first woman to serve
as U.S. Secretary of State, 1997–2001[1]

The Statue of Liberty is one of the great monuments in our nation. It depicts a robed woman representing Libertas (Roman for liberty goddess). Libertas holds a torch above her head with her right hand, and with her left, she carries a tablet with the date July 4, 1776. At her feet lies a broken chain as she walks forward. Over the years, the Statue of Liberty has become an icon of the United States and a welcoming sight to immigrants arriving from around the world.

Immigration has been a hot issue in our country for many years. Unfortunately, there is a lot of misinformation surrounding the topic. Here are some key facts you should know when forming an opinion on the topic of immigration:

1. As a nation, we used to be more welcoming to immigrants than we are today. In 1981, as President Reagan came into office, he faced a refugee crisis with suffering families from Cuba, Vietnam, and Cambodia. Filled with his vintage optimism, Reagan responded to the crisis with these words: "We shall seek new ways to integrate refugees into our society," and he delivered on that promise.[2]

2. Canada has a different approach to immigration than we do. President Obama admitted 12,000 Syrians during the Syrian refugee crisis.[3] Canada, a country with one-tenth of the population of the United States, admitted 40,000. Ahmed Hussen, Canada's immigration minister, said, "We want people to join the Canadian family."[4] Two of the last three governors-general arrived as refugees, one from Haiti and the other from Hong Kong. "Almost one-fifth of Canadians are what people here describe as 'visible minorities'— mostly ethnic Chinese or people with roots in Africa or South Asia— and Muslims constitute three times the percentage of Canadians as Americans. By 2036, almost half of Canadians are expected to be immigrants or children of immigrants," columnist Nicholas Kristof wrote, in a 2017 *New York Times* article.[5]

3. The current reality is that the flow of immigrants who illegally enter the United States has declined dramatically in recent decades—from 1.6 million in 2000 to about 400,000 in 2018, according to U.S. Customs and Border Protection data.[6]

4. A low-growth population trend in the United States will make long-term growth difficult, so we should be more

welcoming to people who want to enter the U.S. legally and become productive citizens. Studies show that immigration boosts productivity and economic growth; restricting it has the opposite effect. Economic output is simply determined by how much each worker produces multiplied by the size of the workforce. The labor force in the United States is not growing as fast as baby boomers are retiring. The U.S. birth rate is now at around 1.9 births per female, well below the replacement level.[7]

5. Immigrants are adding value to the American economy. If you analyzed immigration as an investment, experts would tell you that the American people are making an excellent return on their immigration investment. Farms, restaurants, hotels, manufacturers, retail businesses—all sectors of the economy—benefit directly or indirectly from immigrant labor. Unauthorized immigrants pay sales taxes, property taxes, and gas taxes. The American Action Forum in 2016 estimated that expelling all unauthorized immigrants and keeping them out would cost $400 billion to $600 billion a year and reduce the gross domestic product by $1 trillion.[8]

Immigrants without a Four-year College Degree as a Share of all Workers in Selected Occupations and Industries: March 2018

Farming, fishing, and forestry occupations	36%
Building and grounds cleaning and maintenance occupations	36%
Textile and apparel manufacturing industry	29%
Food manufacturing industry	27%
Accommodation (e.g., hotel) industry	27%
Construction industry	24%
Administrative and support services industry	24%

Source: CBPP analysis of the March 2018 Current Population Survey

International Students Who Became Entrepreneurs of Billion Dollar Companies

Name	University/Degree	Company Co-Founded/ Founded	Employees	Value of Company
Ash Ashutosh	Penn State, M.S. Computer Science	Actifio	350	$1.1 B.
Mohit Aron	Rice, Ph.D. Computer Science	Nutanix	864	$2.0 B.
Alexander Asseily	Stanford, B.S./M.S. Elec. Engineering	Jawbone	395	$3.3 B.
Noubar Afeyan	MIT, Ph.D. Biochemical Engineering Therapeutics	Moderna	326	$3.0 B.
Amr Awadallah	Stanford, Ph.D. Electrical Engineering	Cloudera	1,100	$4.1 B.
Jay Caudhry	Univ. of Cincinnati, MBA and M.S. Computer Engineering, Industrial Engineering	Zscaler	600	$1.1 B.
John Collison	Harvard	Stripe	380	$5.0 B.
Patrick Collison*	MIT	Stripe	(380)	($5.0 B.)
Nicolas Desmarais	Amherst, B.A. Economics & Pol. Science	AppDirect	400	$1.0 B.
Borg Hald	Stanford, MBA, Ross School of Business (U. of Michigan), B.B.A.	Medalia	850	$1.3 B.
David Hindawi	U.C.-Berkeley, Ph.D. Operations Research	Tanium	300+	$3.5 B.
Tomer London	Stanford, M.S. Electrical Engineering Physics, Wharton School (UPENN), B.S. Business	Gusto	300	$1.1 B.
Elon Musk	Univ. of Penn., B.A., Economics &	SpaceX	4,000	$12 B.
Dheeraj Pandey*	Univ. of Texas, Austin, M.S. Computer Science	Nutanix	864	$2.0 B.
Adam Neumann	CUNY Bernard M Baruch College	WeWork	1,200	$10 B.
Dhiraj Rajaram	Wayne State, M.S. Computer Engineering, Univ. of Chicago, MBA	Mu Sigma	3,500	$1.5 B.

Name	University/Degree	Company Co-Founded/ Founded	Employees	Value of Company
Daniel Saks*	Harvard, M.A. Finance & Accounting	AppDirect	(400)	($1.0 B.)
Mario Schlosser	Harvard, MBA Insurance Health	Oscar	415	$1.7 B.
Eric Setton	Stanford, Ph.D. and M.S. Electrical Engineering	Tango	260	$1.0 B.
K.R. Sridhar	University of Illinois at Urbana-Champaign, M.S. Nuclear Energy Engineering, Ph.D. Mechanical Engineering	Bloom	1,200	$2.9 B.
Ragy Thomas	NYU, MBA	Sprinklr	325	$1.2 B.
Renaud Visage	Cornell, M.S. Engineering	Eventbrite	500	$1.0 B.
Michelle Zatlyn	Harvard, MBA	CloudFlare	225	$1.0 B.

Source: National Foundation for American Policy, company information, CrunchBase. *Denotes second international student from same company. Values as of January 1, 2016.

6. Immigrants start new companies at twice the rate of non-immigrants.[9] According to a Pew Research Center report, 31 percent of legal immigrants had earned at least a bachelor's degree—comparable to 32 percent of U.S.-born residents—as of 2017.[10] A new study from the National Foundation for American Policy finds that "55 percent, or 50 of 91 of the country's $1 billion startup companies, had at least one immigrant founder," Stuart Anderson, executive director of the public policy research organization, wrote in a *Forbes* magazine article.[11]

If I am elected president, I will send to Congress in my first 30 days in office the *Statue of Liberty Immigration Act of 2021* based on the facts and based on the reality that immigration has been a key to our success as a nation over the past 240-plus years. Here are key parts of the act:

1. Tighten security along the Mexican border but do not build a wall. As President George W. Bush said in his May 15, 2006, address on immigration: "Our border should be open to trade and lawful immigration, shut to illegal immigrants, as well as criminals, drug dealers, and terrorists."[12] Within my first 30 days in office, I will travel to the U.S.-Mexican border and meet with those in charge of protecting the border. I will listen carefully and make sure that the group in charge of securing the border has all of the tools needed to get the job done. One thing I will not do is build a wall. It is estimated that building a wall will cost $20 billion to $40 billion. Maintaining the wall would be costly, and it is a horrible symbol of the United States across the world. We are known for knocking down walls, not building them. When I asked a Mexican business friend about the wall, he said, "John, we are very good at digging tunnels." A wall or a fence along the entire border with Mexico would be a bad idea because the border is 2,000 miles long, rivers flow through two-thirds of it, and history shows that if people really want to get past a wall, they can.

2. Remove all limits on H-1B visas to attract highly-skilled foreign workers. The United States is an amazing country, and many people around the world want to live here. The H-1B visa program lets companies obtain visas for people with specialized knowledge in fields like biotechnology, computing, engineering, etc. In most cases, H-1B visa applicants must have a bachelor's degree. As president, I will ask Congress to remove all quotas on H-1B visas. I believe it is in the best interest of the United States to recruit super-smart people from around the world and encourage them to live here. We are a nation of immigrants, and by removing limits on H-1B visas, we can attract the best and the brightest from all over the world to help build our country for the future. One former Microsoft employee who was denied an H-1B visa went home to India and started his own company. His name is Kunal Bahl and his company, Snapdeal, an online retailer that competes with Amazon, was worth as much as $7 billion at one point.[13]

3. Streamline the process of becoming an American citizen. As part of the *Statue of Liberty Immigration Act*, I will ask Congress to streamline the process of citizenship. We currently have a great process in place to become an American citizen; it just takes too long. The current process is:

- Get a green card. To get a green card, the qualifications are 1) be at least 18 years old; 2) speak, read, and write English; and 3) be a person of good moral character. This means that you are an upstanding member of society who has a job, pays taxes, and doesn't break the law.

- Satisfy the residency requirements, which include 1) be lawfully admitted to the United States, 2) a resident for five years, and 3) be present in the U.S. for 30 months during those five years.

- Meet the personal requirements. These are the same as those for getting a green card.

- Submit your naturalization papers, pay $640 for an application and $85 for a biometrics (fingerprint) appointment, and pass a civics test by answering six out of 10 questions in English.

This is a great process. The only problem is once you get a green card, you need to wait five years to become an American citizen. I will propose in the *Statue of Liberty Immigration Act* that we reduce the time that someone must hold a green card before applying for citizenship from the current five years to three years. I will propose that we keep the requirement that you must reside in the United States for 30 months.

4. A solution for undocumented immigrants. There are currently 10.5 million illegal immigrants in the United States.[14] I will propose in the *Statue of Liberty Immigration Act* that we allow and encourage a path to citizenship for illegal immigrants if they meet the following criteria:

• Physically present in the United States for five years.

• A person of good moral character for those five years, which means an upstanding member of society who has a job, pays taxes, and doesn't break the law.

• Has not committed a crime.

• Can speak, read, and write English.

As a nation, we have debated immigration for a long time with no resolution. The *Statue of Liberty Immigration Act* will provide a simple, clear, low-cost solution to a difficult problem. It is important to remember that we are a nation of immigrants and that our path to citizenship program only allows quality people who can contribute to the United States to become citizens. For those illegal immigrants who live in America and who meet the criteria, let us grant them a green card and send them on the road to citizenship. The benefits of living up to our immigrant past, increasing the economic vitality of our nation, and taking the moral high ground far outweigh the flat-out lie that immigrants are a drag on our economy and are of low moral character. The time has come to deal with immigration and move on. I have a simple program, and I will provide the leadership to take on immigration and move the country forward. It can be done! ✔

13

Save Social Security

"I am a huge admirer of Franklin Roosevelt's, and I believe Social Security has done untold good in alleviating the once-widespread issue of poverty among the elderly. FDR believed in the greatness and generosity of Americans."

—Jon Meacham, Pulitzer Prize-winning biographer[1]

On August 14, 1935, President Roosevelt signed the Social Security Act. What followed over the next eight decades has been one of our nation's most successful and effective programs. Frank Bane, executive director of the first Social Security Board, said, "The Social Security Act, our first organized nationwide security program, is designed to meet no less than **five** problems:[2]

- Protect childhood
- Provide for the disabled
- Safeguard public health
- Break the impact of unemployment
- Establish a systematic defense against the dependency in old age."

The Social Security program, despite all of its critics, has accomplished most of the goals that President Roosevelt set more than 80 years ago.

While most Americans are aware that Social Security provides a retirement benefit, most people do not understand all of the benefits of Social Security:

1. There are nearly 13 million American children who live in poverty. More than 6.5 million of those children come from homes that receive Social Security benefits.[3]

2. Elderly Americans depend on Social Security. Almost half of the elderly would be poor without Social Security. Currently, the program keeps nearly 15 million elderly Americans out of poverty.[4] Only the top 20 percent of seniors, with incomes above $57,960, do not rely on Social Security as their largest source of income.[5]

3. With fewer American workers who have pension programs in place, Social Security will be a bigger part of the financial future for people who are retiring.

4. Social Security provides disability, medical, and dependent coverage for employees, their spouses, their parents, and their children. Nearly 90 percent of people ages 21 to 64 who worked in 2018 were insured through Social Security in case of disability.[6]

The vast majority of Americans have paid into the Social Security system and are dependent upon its future. When so many are counting on this program in the future, why is it on the brink of bankruptcy?

1. The Social Security system is running out of money. In 2020, it is projected that benefit costs will exceed Social Security tax revenues and trust fund income. In 2035, the trust funds will be depleted, and Social Security will then be able to pay only about 75 cents on the dollar.[7]

2. Demographics are not our friend when it comes to Social Security. The baby boomer generation is retiring, and its effect on Social Security will be massive. By the year 2035, more than 78 million Americans will be 65 or older, up from 56 million today, according to the Social Security Administration. The number of people paying into the system to fund the Social Security payments will fall to 2.3 workers per retiree compared with 2.8 workers per beneficiary today.[8] When Social Security was passed in 1935, giving benefits to those at age 65, the average life expectancy was barely over age 60.[9] Today, the age at which you can receive your full benefits is 66, but life expectancy for men and women is now close to 80.[10] When the program was put into place in 1935, the math made sense. Today, the math makes no sense, and we keep kicking the can of responsibility down the road to the next generation.

3. We have a higher percentage of high-wage earners who do not pay any Social Security taxes over $132,900 of earnings. In 1937, 92 percent of all U.S. earnings were subject to Social Security taxes. Today, 83 percent of earnings fall within the Social Security tax requirement.[11]

4. The birth rate is working against us. Since the 1960s, the birth rate has been in decline.[12] We have fewer young people working to pay for people who are entitled to Social Security. This trend is not going away.

Given the above problems that plague our Social Security system as it is currently administered, how do we fix it? How can we change a system that has done so much for so many and remains a program that millions of Americans are depending on to be there in the future?

If I am elected president, in the first 30 days of my administration, I will propose the *Franklin Roosevelt Social Security Act of 2021*. I propose the following solutions:

1. Scrap the cap. If Congress made one simple change and eliminated Social Security's cap on taxable income, $130 billion in additional money would flow into Social Security every year, according to my estimates. This amount of money would secure the future of this amazing program, which has done so much for so many.

Here's a fair illustration: An assistant to a CEO makes $56,000 a year and pays $3,472 a year in Social Security taxes. The CEO makes $1.2 million or 21.4 times as much as the assistant. The CEO pays a 6.2 percent tax on the first $132,900 of income, or $8,240. The

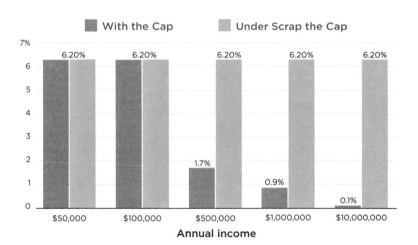

Scrap the Cap

Social Security employee tax as % of income

Source: Social Security Works, Washington | ssworkswa.org

CEO makes 21.4 times more and pays just 2.4 times as much in Social Security taxes. If everyone paid the same percentage, the CEO would be paying $74,400 in Social Security taxes. Scrapping the cap is supported by 80 percent of Americans,[13] and it would make a huge difference in the viability of the program. This is a major tax increase for the top wage earners in our country. Supporting the Scrap the Cap program is one of the things that the top wage earners in this country can do for the good of the country. In the end, there are millions of people who depend on Social Security, and there is a growing divide between the rich and poor in this nation that cannot stand the test of time.

2. Raise the full retirement age. Americans are living longer, yet Social Security rules have not changed to reflect that. When the Social Security program began in 1935, the average American was expected to live to age 61. Today, U.S. average life expectancy is nearly 79 years old.

I propose adopting this option developed by the Congressional Budget Office: The full retirement age would rise from age 67 by two months per birth year, beginning with workers who turn 62 in 2023, until it reaches age 70 for workers born in 1978 or later (who will turn 62 beginning in 2040).[14]

As current law allows, workers could still choose to start receiving reduced benefits at age 62, but the reduction in their monthly payments would be larger. For example, for those born in 1978, if they decide to start taking Social Security benefits at age 62, their payments would be 45 percent less than if they wait until they turn 70, under the CBO plan.

This option would shrink federal payouts by $28 billion through 2028. By 2048, the plan would decrease Social Security outlays under the current law by 8 percent or approximately $92 billion per year, by my estimate, and put Social Security on firm financial footing for the rest of the century.

3. Reform the Social Security disability program. The disability program offered through Social Security should be reformed by requiring those who are eligible for disability payments to reapply for the program every two years. Calls for reform have described this program as a "secret welfare system" with its own "disability industrial complex" ravaged by waste and fraud.

Percentage Distribution of Household Income in the United States in 2018

Annual household income in U.S. dollars

Percentage of U.S. households

Under 15,000	10.2%
15,000 to 24,999	8.9%
25,000 to 34,999	8.8%
35,000 to 49,999	12%
50,000 to 74,999	17.2%
75,000 to 99,999	12.5%
100,000 to 149,999	14.9%
150,000 to 199,999	7%
200,000 and over	8.5%

Source: Statista

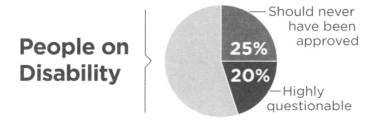

People on Disability

25% —Should never have been approved

20%

—Highly questionable

Former Senator Tom Coburn, a physician who was the ranking Republican on the Senate Subcommittee for Investigations, conducted a study in 2013 and concluded that 25 percent of people on disability should never have been approved, while another 20 percent were highly questionable.[15] Putting people on disability who should not be on disability is costing our country billions of dollars. According to the study, along the Kentucky-West Virginia border, more than a quarter of a million people were on disability, which translates into 10 to 15 percent of the population—approximately three times higher than the national average. Even worse is that in 2015, "the Social Security Administration paid a billion dollars to claimants' lawyers out of its ... disability trust fund." Seventy million dollars "went to ... the largest disability law firm in the country."[16] Yes, you, the taxpayer, paid $70 million to one law firm to get people onto disability. A great nation does not let people take advantage of the system. Taxpayers should not be paying for people who do not need to be on disability, and we should not be paying outrageous sums to lawyers who are encouraging citizens to apply for disability and cheat the system.

Social Security is an amazing program. It provides a retirement program for the vast majority of American seniors, and it provides disability coverage for most American workers and their families. When we talk about the growing income inequality in America, Social Security is one program that provides an income for many of our older residents and a safety net for all American workers. While this great program has helped hundreds of millions since its inception in 1935, it is hanging by a financial thread. All we need to do is show some leadership and make three simple changes, and Social Security will be fixed for the next 100 years. ✔

14

Simplify the Tax Code

> "The hardest thing in the world to understand is the income tax."
>
> —Albert Einstein, Nobel Prize-winning physicist[1]

People don't like to pay taxes—they never have and they never will. Unfortunately, reducing taxes has become an American political sport. We love to reduce taxes without reducing spending. This is how you get elected in America: "I will cut your taxes, and I will cut ridiculous government spending." Taxes are cut, and no one ever cuts the ridiculous spending. Revenue goes down, spending stays the same while the debt continues to climb, and we now have a $23 trillion debt that we are going to kick down the road to our kids. It's a great way to get elected, but a lousy way to run a country.

The Trump tax cuts of 2017 promised to achieve three things: 1) to be revenue neutral, meaning they would not add to the deficit; 2) to be simple; and 3) to be fair. What actually happened: The 2017 tax program is expected to add $1.8 trillion to $1.9 trillion to the deficit over the next 10 years.[2] The bill itself is almost 1,100 pages long,[3] and more than 60 percent of the benefits go to the top 20 percent of taxpayers.[4] Mayor John Hamilton of Bloomington, Indiana, wrote, in an editorial for *The Washington Post* in opposition to the 2017 Republican tax cuts, "If I asked the city council to approve tripling our local debt to give hundreds of thousands of dollars per year to a few hundred of our most prosperous residents, they would ask me what I was smoking. Preposterous, they would say."[5] That's exactly what we did at the federal level.

In fact, the richest 400 families in the U.S. now pay a lower tax rate than the average working-class family. A study by University of California-Berkeley economists Emmanuel Saez and Gabriel Zucman shows that in 2018—for the first time in history—the 400 wealthiest American families paid an average effective tax rate of 23 percent, while the bottom half of U.S. households paid an average effective rate of 24.2 percent.[6] That includes federal, state, local, and corporate taxes as well as what the economists called "indirect taxes," such as vehicle and business licenses. By comparison, in 1980, the richest households had an effective tax rate of 47 percent, and in 1960, they paid as much as 56 percent, while the effective tax rate for lower earners has held steady over the years, a *Washington Post* story said.[7]

While we hate taxes, we have lost sight of the fact that the money we pay in taxes provides us with significant benefits. Even though there are massive opportunities to reduce government spending, we get real value from our tax dollars. Here are a few examples of what your tax dollars support:

- **Running our government.** It's easy to forget that our government has employees and offices, and tax dollars are needed to support this. These are the people we count on to protect our nation, react to natural disasters, to keep our nation healthy by approving or disapproving new drugs, to run and maintain our national parks, to maintain our transportation system, and to educate our children, just to name a few expenditures that your tax dollars pay for.

- **Public utilities and transportation.** The only reason we can drive our cars is because of taxes our government uses to plan and build our roads and bridges. Without government taxes, we would not have all of our roads, bridges and airports. Without taxes, America stops moving.

- **Education.** Nearly 90 percent of students attend public schools.[8] Our public schools and our public universities receive a significant portion of their funding from the federal government. Without it, our public education system would be a shell of what it is today.

- **Public safety.** Your taxes pay for police and firefighters—basic services that most Americans take for granted.

- **The public safety net.** The vast majority of Americans can take care of themselves, yet unfortunately, millions of Americans face challenges that they cannot deal with alone. They suffer from mental illness, poverty, health problems, or other issues. They need help, and the government, through Social Security, Medicaid, and SNAP (Supplemental Nutrition Assistance Program, formerly food stamps), steps in to help people in need. In reality, our tax dollars are helping people who cannot help themselves.

- **National security.** Our national defense, which is paid for with our taxes, has served us well during wartime and peacetime. The national defense has been called upon during the past 100 years for World War I, World War II, the Cold War, the Korean War, the Vietnam conflict, both Iraqi engagements, in Afghanistan, the "War on Terror," and so much more. More importantly, the investment in our military has sent a message: Don't mess with the United States. The United States is the most powerful nation in the world because our taxes pay for it. No taxes, no powerful military, no security. Without a powerful U.S. military, we would live in a much different world.

Our federal government does a horrible job marketing itself. We don't hear about the essential programs it runs that help our families every day. Everyone likes to take potshots at Washington but in reality, our government does a lot of great things, and they need to be paid for … through taxes. Taxes are dues that we pay to be members of the club. In our case, the club is to be a citizen of the United States, the greatest nation in the history of the world. Former U.S. Supreme Court Justice Oliver Wendell Holmes Jr. said, "I like to pay taxes. With them, I buy civilization."[9] You might not like to pay taxes, but we need to understand that without taxes, our country does not function.

It is my opinion that the one big problem we have in our country when it comes to taxes is not the amount we pay—it is that the current tax code is a complete joke, and it is the best illustration that our nation's government is broken. Congress is responsible for the tax code, and it is perhaps the worst piece of legislation ever created. No one has dared to change the tax code because the few who benefit from its complexity have so much more money and power than the average Americans who have neither the wealth nor the power to change it.

Here are the reasons why our current system is not working:

1. The current tax code is too complicated. Our tax law is 2,652 pages long. In 1913, it was 400 pages.[10] The current tax code is lucrative for tax lawyers but bad for America.

General Electric, one of the largest corporations in America, filed a 57,000-page federal tax return for 2011 and ended up paying zero in taxes on $14 billion in profit.[11] General Electric has done nothing wrong; it just has the right accountants and lawyers who can figure out how to pay *zero* while making $14 billion.

Apple held $246 billion offshore—more than any other company—to avoid paying $76.7 billion in U.S. taxes, according to 2017 studies by the U.S. Public Interest Research Group and the Institute on Taxation and Economic Policy.[12] Citigroup reported $47 billion held in other countries on which it would owe $13.1 billion in U.S. taxes, and Goldman Sachs held $31.2 billion offshore.[13]

Fortune 500 companies socked away more than $2.6 trillion in accumulated profits offshore for tax purposes, the reports said, avoiding as much as $752 billion in U.S. income taxes.[14]

Since the 2017 tax law gave tax breaks to corporations for returning those overseas stashes, Apple has said it would transfer back nearly all of its offshore money.[15] In all, American companies have returned more than $1 trillion to the U.S.[16]

Even so, former Republican Senator Tom Coburn described our current system well when he said, "The biggest breaks go to corporations and individuals who can afford the best lobbyists, lawyers and accountants, leaving everyday Americans to fill the gap."[17]

2. The tax code changes all the time. From 2001 through 2012, there were nearly 5,000 alterations, or an average of one change per day.[18] How can you keep up with a game whose rules switch once a day? Imagine if the NFL changed its rules once a day.

3. The current tax code is expensive and eats up resources of both the U.S. government and its people. It is so complicated that Americans spend $168 billion a year either to hire a professional to do their taxes or for software to calculate their returns on their own.[19]

4. There are too many loopholes in the current tax code. For example, Exxon paid $1.1 billion to settle its disastrous oil spill in Alaska in 1989. Because of the tax code, Exxon was able to deduct about half the cost. Corporate jets receive faster depreciation rates than commercial airlines because of a tax loophole, and NASCAR is able to depreciate tracks over seven years when the government estimates that tracks really depreciate over 39 years.[20]

According to *Forbes* magazine, using names like Find the Children, The Veterans Fund, and Cancer Fund of America, people and organizations take advantage of the nonprofit tax deduction. The Cancer Fund of America spent less than 1 percent of its donations on charitable giving, and over 10 years, it paid its founders over $5 million, according to the *Forbes* article.[21] "Despite millions in profits, the NFL, the NHL, and the PGA tour are classified as nonprofits, exempting their earnings from federal income tax," the *Forbes* article said.[22] The list goes on and on. The tax system makes no strategic sense. It has been cobbled together by politicians who have been influenced by big money over the past 50 years. It is the opposite of good wine. It keeps getting worse with time. As an example, in 2018, according to the Institute on Taxation and Economic Policy, 60 of the Fortune 500 companies paid ZERO taxes on $79 billion in profits.[23]

5. Tax breaks are really government expenditures. The reality of the current system is that top earners received an average tax cut of $66,384 in 2011, while the bottom 20 percent saw a tax break of $107.[24] With the 2017 tax reform, Americans on the lowest end of the pay scale received a benefit of about $60 in 2018 while middle class households saw an average tax break of $930. Meanwhile, the top 0.1 percent—those with an average annual adjusted gross income of $7.3 million or more—had an average gain of $193,380, according to an analysis by the Tax Policy Center.[25]

Most people see tax deductions as taxes they don't have to pay. While that is true, tax breaks can also be considered government spending. There is no difference between $100 that the government spends on a program and $100 that the government gives as a tax break.

If I am elected president, I will propose to Congress within 30 days the *Tax Simplification Act of 2021*. The *Tax Simplification Act* will be a five-step plan to bring simplicity, clarity, and fairness to our tax code. Here are the keys to the plan:

1. I will propose that we simplify the tax code from 2,652 pages to 10 pages. I will give the American people a tax code they can understand and a tax code that works for the people, not the special interest groups. My proposed 10-page code will be simple and straightforward, and all Americans will know what the rules of the game are.

2. Significantly reduce the number of tax breaks by adopting the Bowles-Simpson Tax Recommendation.[26] The proposal will eliminate all tax breaks except the child credit, earned income tax credit for very low-income earners, foreign tax credits for taxes paid abroad, employer-sponsored health insurance reduced rates, charitable-giving deduction, retirement savings reduced rates, and mortgage interest reduced rates. Everything else goes, and this is how we get down to a simple tax code that is understandable and levels the playing field for all Americans.

3. Tax capital gains and dividends at normal tax rates. Both capital gains and dividends are income, just like a salary or an hourly wage. Simplify the tax code, and call all income "earned income."

Tax it all the same. I am estimating that this simple change would raise $40 billion a year in revenue.

4. Eliminate all corporate tax breaks and leave the rate at 21 percent. The Trump tax plan reduced the corporate rate to 21 percent so U.S. companies could be globally competitive. Some of the tax breaks that corporations received were eliminated to finance the rate reduction. In the *Tax Simplification Act of 2021*, I will ask Congress to eliminate all corporate tax breaks. The government should not be in the business of picking winners and losers in the market. Why should oil companies get big tax breaks, while running shoe companies do not? Why should certain farmers get big tax subsidies, while other farmers get nothing? Our tax system is overly complicated, and we should simplify it by getting out of the business of letting members of Congress pick winners and losers with the tax code. If the U.S. government wants to help a certain industry because it is in the best interests of the people of the United States, then that industry should get a subsidy, and it should be put in a budget so that everyone can see what the subsidy is, how much it costs the people of the United States, and that the subsidy has a time limit. We need to get out of the business of letting politicians and lawyers bury hundreds of billions of dollars' worth of benefits for special interests that last forever in our 2,652-page document called the tax code.

When the Trump tax cuts were passed and the published corporate rate was reduced to 21 percent, the average Fortune 500 company actually paid 11 percent, after deductions, in 2018.[27] My plan would have every company in America paying 21 percent. This would level the playing field and raise $96 billion a year, by my estimates, and significantly reduce our annual deficit.

5. Have the IRS send out a pre-filled tax return, complete with all of the relevant information. As described by Harvard Law School professor Cass R. Sunstein, this approach is called the simple return and has been proposed by Austan Goolsbee, former chairman of the Council of Economic Advisers.[28] All you would need to do is review the information and sign it. The entire process would take five minutes to complete. California has experimented with this process,[29] and as many as three dozen countries—including Denmark, Sweden, Germany, Japan and the United Kingdom—offer some form of return-free tax filing.[30] If I am elected president, we will have a simple return option ready to go within 12 months. The government exists to serve the people, and eliminating the estimated 10 hours the average person spends on calculating tax returns is something simple that the government can do for its citizens.

Under the *Tax Simplification Act of 2021*, the American people will realize the following benefits:

- I am estimating that this plan would generate more than $150 billion in additional revenue per year and would significantly close our budget gap. We cannot continue to spend significantly more money than we take in. This tax plan would do what Congress has been unable to do: simplify the tax code and significantly increase revenues.

- We would bring some sense of fairness and logic to the tax code. We could take the tax code of 2,652 pages and reduce it to fewer than 10 pages. Americans would actually understand the rules of the game. The simple tax code would also help level the playing field between the rich and the poor.

- This would simplify people's lives. I estimate that the amount of time to fill out a tax form would be reduced by 98 percent. Many of the people who are employed in America to deal with taxes, including tax accountants, employees of the IRS, and tax attorneys, could be freed up to do something that adds value to the United States and its people.

There is no greater example of how poorly our country is being run than the current tax system. Many presidents have been elected by promising to cut taxes and spending. They cut the taxes and never find the spending cuts they promise. I am a different kind of candidate. I believe that with a $23 trillion deficit, and running almost a $1 trillion deficit per year, we cannot cut taxes. I will work harder than any president to cut expenses, but at the same time, we need to increase taxes on the wealthiest Americans.

If you are interested in having a tax code that you can understand, spending significantly less time preparing your tax returns, and if you believe the wealthiest Americans should not be able to use a complicated tax code to avoid paying taxes, then I am your candidate. My plan will deliver a simple, fair, and honest tax code for the American people. ✓

15

Reform Campaign Finance

"The number one lobby that opposes campaign finance reform in the United States is the National Association of Broadcasters."

—Robert W. McChesney, author and professor
of communication at the University of Illinois[1]

A simple tenet of a true democracy is one person, one vote. No one's vote should count more than anyone else's. The Pew Research Center reports that 74 percent of the American public believes that major donors should not have more influence than regular citizens.[2] If the opposite happens and major donors hold more power in elections than the average voter, then the game is rigged, and over time, people will stop playing. And over time, the democracy that we have built over 240 years will fall apart.

In the United States, money has infiltrated our political process to the point that the determining factor in who wins a campaign is not who is the most competent candidate or who has the best ideas; it is who has been able to raise the largest amount of money. People do not give massive amounts of money to politicians for the good of the country. They give massive amounts of money to politicians to obtain influence, and they expect favors in return.

In 2015, former President Jimmy Carter said the United States is an "oligarchy" in which "unlimited political bribery" has created "a complete subversion of our political system as a payoff to major contributors."[3]

What evidence exists to support the theory that money in politics is out of control and that the core principle of our democracy is in danger? Consider the following:

1. Elections are won by the highest bidder. Since 2000, more than 85 percent of the candidates for House seats who spent more money won their elections. Of the Senate contenders, at least 75 percent of the big spenders were the winners in every election since 2000, except 2006 when 73 percent of them won.[4]

2. The rising cost of elections is out of control and getting worse with time. In 2012, candidates for the U.S. Senate raised an average of $10.47 million for their campaigns. Elizabeth Warren led the pack, drawing $42.5 million for her successful run for the Massachusetts seat. Candidates for the U.S. House raised an average $1.7 million in 2012.[5] In the 2016 Pennsylvania Senate race between Republican Pat Toomey and Democratic challenger Katie McGinty, $164 million was spent. Where did all the money come from? Only 28 percent of the money came directly from the candidates' campaigns. Over $100 million was spent on the race by groups based outside the state of Pennsylvania.[6]

In the 2016 Nevada Senate race, Democrat Catherine Cortez Masto spent almost $19 million. Her opponent, Republican Joe Heck, spent nearly $12 million. Together, they pumped over $30 million into the

Cost of Elections

Cycle	Total Cost of Election	Congressional Races	Presidential Race
2016	$6,511,181,587	$4,124,304,874	$2,386,876,712
2012	$6,285,557,223	$3,664,141,430	$2,621,415,792
2008	$5,285,680,883	$2,485,952,737	$2,799,728,146
2004	$4,147,304,003	$2,237,073,141	$1,910,230,862
2000	$3,082,340,937	$1,669,224,553	$1,413,116,384

Source: OpenSecrets.org

battle to succeed Democratic minority leader Harry Reid, who retired after 30 years in the Senate. Unfortunately, outside groups outspent the candidates by pouring more than $88 million into the Nevada contest.[7]

Then, the 2018 U.S. Senate race in Florida broke new territory for spending. Republican Rick Scott's campaign poured a record $83.5 million into the contest, including a record $63.5 million from Scott himself.[8] Total spending on that race, which Scott narrowly won, topped $209 million—for one Senate seat!![9]

3. The wealthy wield more financial clout. "In 1980, the richest one-hundredth of 1 percent of Americans provided 10 percent of contributions to federal elections. By 2012, they provided 40 percent," wrote former U.S. Secretary of Labor Robert B. Reich, in his book, *The Common Good*.[10]

In the 2018 elections, those who contributed at least $1 million accounted for 74 percent of the $1.1 billion that poured into super PACS—political action committees that cannot fund individual candidates or political parties but can make unlimited political expenditures, independently.[11]

4. Today's politicians spend as much as 50 percent of their time raising money for the next election, up from 10 to 15 percent in the 1980s and 1990s, said Nick Penniman, CEO of Issue One, which describes itself as a "crosspartisan" political reform group.[12] Would we rather have our public servants representing the people and attending to the nation's business or raising money?

If I am elected president, in my first week on the job, I will propose the *Campaign Finance Reform Act of 2021*. It will call for a constitutional amendment that incorporates the following two simple solutions to significantly reduce the influence of money on our political process:

1. Eliminate any campaign contributions to candidates from businesses, unions, or any other organizations, including political action committees. The only contributions allowed will be from people who are actually eligible to vote. We don't let businesses, PACs, or unions vote, so why do we let them donate money and influence elections?

2. Prohibit out-of-state money in state elections. It is ridiculous that someone from California can make a donation to a candidate running for governor in Nebraska, and yet it happens all the time. Out-of-state individuals are giving significant amounts of money to candidates in states where they do not reside. Do you want someone outside of your state supporting candidates in your state and having the ability to influence the outcome of the election?

The benefits of asking Congress to pass a constitutional amendment to ban out-of-state money in state elections and to ban campaign contributions from people and organizations who cannot vote in those races would be the following:

- **Presidents, governors, and members of Congress would be able to spend significantly more of their time doing their jobs instead of raising money for the next election.** The productivity of our highest-ranking public officials would go through the roof.

- **Government officials would not owe favors to big-money contributors.** More decisions would be made in the best interests of the United States and its citizens and less in paying off the big contributors. One of the reasons why we have such a large income gap in the United States is because fewer people make a higher percentage of political contributions. Those people who are making the large campaign donations then ask for legislation that favors their pocketbooks.

The flood of political donations from sources such as health care companies and defense contractors would evaporate, leaving government officials to make decisions that are in the best interests of the country.

- **The current ability of mega-contributors to buy elections would come to an end.** Rich donors, corporations, and unions could no longer influence elections with massive contributions, and every citizen's vote would be equal. This would restore people's belief in our democracy.

Fred Wertheimer, former president of Common Cause and founder of the nonprofit Democracy 21, said in a 2014 article in *The New Yorker*, "We have three elements today: unlimited contributions, corporate money, and secret money. Those were the three elements of Watergate."[13] And as Harvard professor Lawrence Lessig said, "Today we can do legally everything Nixon had to do illegally."[14]

In *The Federalist Papers #52*, James Madison wrote: "The door of this part of the federal government is open to merit of every description; whether native or adoptive, whether young or old, and without regard for poverty or wealth, or to any particular profession of religious faith."[15] Madison would cringe if he were alive today. The door of the federal government is 100 times more open to politically active people with a lot of money than it is to the average American.

We have a great opportunity to put an end to the days when the few govern the many.

The constitutional amendment that I will ask Congress to pass will eliminate campaign contributions from organizations that cannot vote and will put an end to people influencing elections in states where they do not reside. These changes will be very difficult because those who want to stop reform will pay an enormous amount of money to achieve that. These two simple solutions will take a massive amount of cash out of politics and will result in better decision-making that will be in the best interests of the American people.

I will practice what I preach. In my campaign, I will not accept any money from businesses, unions, or PACs. I will only accept money from people who can vote. ✓

16

Create an Economy Built to Last

"When making choices, or setting policies about the economy, education, or medicine, society is best served by electing people who are particularly hardworking, intelligent, and interested in long-term thinking."

—Bill Gates

One of the main responsibilities of the president is to provide leadership for the economy. Presidents can create the environment to create jobs, but at the end of the day, people and companies create the vast majority of jobs. Too often, the presidential candidates' economic plans can be summed up as cutting taxes and reducing government spending. The tax cuts happen, and the reduction in government spending never does. This is why, as a nation, we now have a $23 trillion debt.

According to *The Balance*, President Donald Trump's proposed budget for the 2021 fiscal year would bring the increase in the national debt to $4.8 trillion for his first term. If he wins a second term, the debt would jump by $8.3 trillion over the eight years, to a total of $28.5 trillion, according to his administration's estimates. During the 2016 campaign, Trump had promised to **eliminate** the debt within eight years.[1]

At some point in the future, we will face an economic meltdown if we continue with the tax cuts that make voters happy and pass on the spending cuts, which have resulted in the massive debt that we have today, and that our children will have to pay off tomorrow.

If I am elected president, my economic plan will not be a short-term plan based on tax cuts and mysterious spending cuts that never happen. My economic plan will be the sum of all the plans I have put

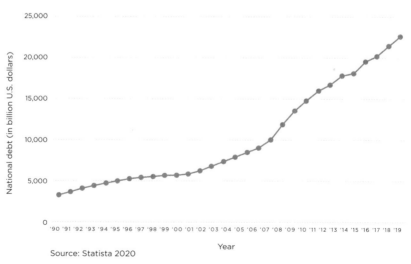

Public Debt of the United States from 1990 to 2019

in billions U.S. dollars

Source: Statista 2020

forth in this book. By implementing these policies, we will be laying the foundation for long-term, sustainable economic growth that will benefit all Americans.

Here is a summary of the plans discussed in this book and the impact they will have on building a strong economy for the future:

1. Create a high-performance government. In presidential campaigns, too little time is spent discussing the government and how it runs. I am proposing more changes to the way the government is run than any candidate in the last 100 years by making sure we focus on our biggest problems no matter how difficult they might be, having the best employees in every position, creating a great place to work, and providing clear direction through the proven objectives and key results process, to name a few. These improvements will increase productivity and reduce the overall cost of government. This will be good for the economy.

2. Take the global lead on climate change. Over the past 140 years, the average surface temperature on our planet has risen 2 degrees, NASA scientists say. Since 1958, the amount of carbon in our atmosphere has jumped by more than 30 percent. In 2017, the amount of damage from climate change-related catastrophes in the United States reached a record $306 billion. I have a plan to take a global leadership role to address climate change, and by doing so, it will significantly benefit the economy over the long term.

3. Reduce the nuclear arsenal from 6,185 nuclear weapons in 2018 to around 300. This plan will significantly reduce our defense spending and protect us from a "black swan" event. How much do you think it would cost our economy if we were involved in a nuclear war? Ninety percent of wars throughout human history were caused by miscommunication. My plan to reduce the nuclear arsenal is good for the economy.

4. Fix the health care system. We currently spend $3.65 trillion a year on health care, the most money in the world by far, and we get the worst results. My health care plan will significantly reduce the cost of our health care system. The plan will also significantly improve the overall health of the American people. Healthy people are significantly more productive than unhealthy people, and that is good for the economy. A significant reduction in health care costs will be an incentive for employers to hire more workers and will make American companies more competitive in the global marketplace.

5. Increase the gas tax to $1 a gallon and implement the *Eisenhower Two Transportation Act of 2021*, a massive infrastructure plan to rebuild America. Our infrastructure is rated a D+ and needs help. My plan to rebuild America will put millions of people to work in high-paying jobs that will help the economy. Paying for it by raising the gas tax is the fiscally prudent thing to do. Improving our infrastructure from a D+ to an A will significantly improve our transportation system, which will provide a great foundation for the American economy for the next 50 years.

6. Increase opportunity in America. I will propose to Congress the *Every Kid Has a Chance Program*. This program will address the nearly 13 million children who live below the poverty line and, unfortunately, are all too often destined to a bleak future of poor education, unemployment, and for many, significant prison time. These kids come into society without a chance, and many end up becoming a drain on society because they are unemployed or in jail, or both. My plan will invest in these kids upfront so they can become productive, taxpaying adults in the future. Investing in kids who are in poverty when they are young is a cheap investment compared to paying for unemployment and prison costs later in life. Meanwhile, raising the minimum wage to $15 will help lift families out of poverty—now.

7. Fix Congress. I am proposing term limits, waiving the pay of members of Congress with more than $10 million net worth, eliminating congressional pensions, and giving the president the line item veto. These actions will lead to a more productive Congress. The line-item veto will lead to greater financial discipline, and Congress will do a more effective job at a lower cost. All of this will be good for the economy.

8. Cut defense spending. In 2019, we spent $1 trillion on defense. We spend more money on defense than the next eight nations combined, according to the Stockholm International Peace Research Institute, and we outspend the Russians by more than 16 to one! Russia spends $61.4 billion, SIPRI figures show.[2] My plan is to reduce defense spending to $750 billion a year by the second year of my administration and save $250 billion per year. Reduced government spending and a lower deficit are good for the long-term economy.

9. Deliver a more effective American foreign policy. My administration will use diplomacy to live up to the mission of the State Department, which is "to advance freedom for the benefit of the American people and the international community." We will do this by making friends around the world. When we do this, we will open new markets to American products, and we will also build the American brand. A sound foreign policy can have a positive impact on trade, tourism, and many other facets of the economy. My administration will work hard to make friends around the world, and by doing so, we will expand economic opportunity.

10. Reduce gun violence in America. My plan is to reduce gun violence by 90 percent. I know this can happen because Western countries that are similar to the United States but have different gun laws have 90 percent fewer gun deaths and injuries than we do. The nearly 40,000 people who die from gunshots in a year—including more than 14,000 homicide victims—and the 100,000 who are wounded by guns every year cost the American economy over $200 billion a year. Having similar gun laws that every other Western country has will be good for the economy.

11. Fix the legal system and reduce our prison population. I will send to Congress a bill to adopt the English Rule of Law, whereby if a person decides to sue another person and loses, the losing plaintiff is responsible for all court costs. This will wipe out at least 50 percent of the ridiculous lawsuits in America and will make the United States a much better place to do business. Making America a better place to do business will grow the economy. I also have a plan to cut the prison population in half within five years. We currently have 2.3 million Americans locked up in jails, equating to 655 Americans per 100,000 people. My plan to sharply reduce that number will benefit the economy in two ways. First, the cost savings will be at least $30 billion a year. Second, we will have 1 million more people available to work and to be consumers. This will be another plus for the economy.

12. Build our economy through immigration. Immigrants have been a huge engine of growth throughout American history. The size of any economy is the number of people multiplied by their productivity. Believe it or not, our government is doing its best to keep super-smart people out of our country. I will, in an organized manner, welcome immigrants to America if they meet our immigration standards. By doing this, we will use immigration to build our economy.

13. Fix Social Security. Social Security is a program that is hanging by a financial thread. My program to scrap the cap and have people pay the same percentage of their paycheck into Social Security, regardless of their income, will save and strengthen this program. In 2019, nearly 64 million Americans received a Social Security check.[3] A fiscally stable Social Security program is good for the economy.

14. Simplify the tax code. Today, we have a tax code that is 2,652 pages long and contains $1.1 trillion of loopholes.[4] As president, I will set a goal to reduce the tax code to 10 pages. A simplified tax code will simplify the game and encourage more people to play. A simplified tax code will also lead to more people and companies paying their fair share of taxes, which will bring the deficit down, which is also good for the long-term economy.

15. Reform campaign finance. My proposals for eliminating any campaign contributions from businesses, unions, or political action committees will take the power away from special interest groups that are buying political influence and will swing the balance of power to politicians who can make decisions in the best interest of the country. Today, the vast majority of key decision-makers in our government receive campaign contributions that could be influencing their votes.

Implementing my campaign finance reform plan will allow lawmakers to focus on making the best long-term decisions for the United States, and that will benefit the economy.

Giving big tax cuts and piling onto the $23 trillion deficit that we have amassed is an easy way to grow the economy in the short term. The problem is that at the end of the day, your children will be paying for that deficit. Leadership is taking a position and explaining to people why it is in their best interest to follow. It is my belief that as a country, we have become too fixated on tax cuts and interest rate cuts as a cure for whatever economic woes we have. To grow the economy over the long term, we need to take on the hard issues and make the difficult choices. I have a simple, bold plan to build our economy for the long term. ✔

Conclusion

> "The only thing necessary for the triumph
> of evil is for good men to do nothing."
>
> —Edmund Burke the Irish Philosopher[1]

Tom Brokaw wrote a book titled *The Greatest Generation*.[2] In his book, Brokaw wrote that the generation of people who grew up in the United States during the Great Depression and then went on to fight in World War II and to support the home effort was the Greatest Generation. He argued that these men and women fought not for fame and recognition, but because it was the right thing to do.

Those of us born after the Greatest Generation are not leaving our nation in better shape for our children and future generations. The good news is that there is an amazing opportunity to step up and solve these major issues.

I am running for president because I believe that as a nation, we are at a crossroads. One path leads to more of the same: politicians putting their party and their careers ahead of the country, decisions being influenced by big money, and not much getting done in Washington, D.C. The second path is the road less traveled. It is Republicans,

Democrats, Independents and all others coming together and putting the country first and making sacrifices to solve the major problems that we face. Just like Americans during World War II, we are faced with a crisis, and just as they took action, we can do something about it, or we can sit on the sidelines and hope for better times ahead.

Think about what we could accomplish as a country in the next four years:

1. We could be the generation to create a high-performance government. How can you have a high-performance team when you can't fire the poor performers? It cannot be done. Why do we tolerate a poorly performing government when we, the people, own the government? Focus on the tough issues with the biggest impact on people, abolish government unions, make the federal government a great place to work, and give the power back to the people. It is a decision that will be in the best interests of the United States.

2. We could be the first generation to address climate change. Over the last 140 years, the temperature on earth has increased by two degrees, which is causing massive environmental problems all over the globe. In 2017, the cost of extreme weather events in the United States was $306 billion. We are the second-largest polluter in the world, and the global environment continues to get worse. If we don't do anything, the future of every human on this planet looks bleak. As a nation, we have helped to win two world wars, we kept the peace during the Cold War, we put the first man on the moon, and we have lifted more people out of poverty than any nation in history. If we want to fix the environment, we can do it.

3. We could be the generation to rid the world of nuclear weapons. We should be scared stiff over the number of nuclear weapons that exist in the world and the high probability of a nuclear accident over time, and of the ability of terrorist organizations to acquire nuclear weapons. It is time for America to take a global leadership role in reducing the chance for nuclear Armageddon. We can clean up our own house first and be an example to the rest of the world. Reduce our arsenal from 6,185 active missiles to around 300. Pledge to the world that we will not use our nuclear forces as a first-strike option. We could be the generation to bring the nuclear age under control and take the first major step since the advent of the nuclear age to bring it to an end.

4. We could be the generation to fix the health care system. We are the unhealthiest population in the history of America. We could be the generation that looks at ourselves in the mirror and says, "The health of our people is poor, and our health care system is out of control. We are going to fix it." With some bold decisions, this generation could significantly increase the health of our citizens and decrease the cost of the most expensive health care system in the world.

5. We could be the generation that rebuilds America's infrastructure by raising the gas tax to $1 a gallon. By raising the gas tax, we could take America's infrastructure, which is currently rated a D+, and make it the envy of the world. What Eisenhower did in the 1950s with building the interstate system, this generation could do for the 21st century. We have great ideas on how to get it done and absolutely no political will to find the funds to build an infrastructure for future generations that could make America more competitive, increase our quality of living, and put millions of Americans to work. This generation could be the generation to rebuild America.

6. We could be the generation to increase opportunity for all Americans. Over the last 30 years, America's famous middle class has shrunk, and our citizens at the bottom of the ladder have less hope for the future. With a few bold moves, we could reduce childhood poverty by 50 percent and give every kid a chance to achieve the American dream.

7. We could be the generation to reorganize our government and make significant changes in the way Congress operates and fix the gridlock in Washington. We could have citizen legislators instead of professional politicians running our government. We could orchestrate the most significant structural changes in our government since the Founding Fathers.

8. We could be the generation that honors President Eisenhower by curtailing the military-industrial complex. We spend more money on defense than the next eight nations combined. Much of it is warranted, yet much of it is not. The time has come to spend less on defense so we can pay our bills.

9. We could be the generation that fixes America's foreign policy. We could be the generation that once again takes a leadership role in the world. There are major international problems that need to be addressed like climate change, nuclear proliferation, and the global economy, to name a few. We can take a leadership role to make sure these issues are addressed, and the beneficiaries of a sound foreign policy of the United States will be freedom-loving countries all over the world.

10. We could be the generation to implement sensible gun laws so that guns will not take the lives of nearly 40,000 Americans or leave another 100,000 wounded every year. We can do all of this and still let responsible, proud gun owners use their guns to go hunting and to protect themselves at home.

11. We could be the generation to fix our legal system. We have four times the number of lawsuits per person than our friends in Canada, and we imprison more people than anyone in the world. We have more than 2.3 million people in prisons all across America— that translates to 655 per 100,000 people. In the 1970s, that number was just over 100. We could be the generation that puts the people first and the lawyers second and creates more legal reform in one year than the amount of reform enacted over the last 200 years.

12. We could be the generation that solves the immigration crisis in America. We are a nation of immigrants, and one of our most powerful national symbols is the Statue of Liberty, welcoming immigrants to our great nation. We could be the generation that attracts highly skilled foreign workers to become American citizens, knowing that smart immigrants moving to America can create jobs, increase the tax base, and add to the social fabric of our nation. We could be the generation that finds a solution for the 10.5 million undocumented immigrants in our country. If an illegal immigrant is a person of good moral character, has a job, pays taxes, has not committed a crime, and can speak, read, and write English, we should put these immigrants on a fast path to citizenship.

13. We could be the generation that saves Social Security. An amazing program that has done so much for so many hangs by a thread because Congress won't deal with it. We could make sure that Social Security is a solid program that every American can count on for the future.

14. We could be the generation to fix the tax code. Our politicians have piled up a tax code of 2,652 pages. We could be the generation to put an end to the madness and have a 10-page tax code that all Americans can understand.

15. We could be the generation to reform campaign finance. More than three-fourths of political candidates who raise the largest amount of money win. We allow individuals with great wealth to give candidates unlimited money to buy elections. In the United States, elections should not be for sale. We should not be putting elected officials into office based on who is the best fundraiser. We should be putting people into office based on who has the best capabilities for the job and who has the best ideas. We could eliminate campaign contributions from corporations and unions, and prohibit money from out-of-state contributors in local elections. We could be the generation that takes down the "For Sale" sign next to the White House and the Capitol.

16. We could be the generation that builds a strong economic foundation for years to come by making long-term decisions. Addressing issues like our crumbling infrastructure, Social Security, childhood poverty, and immigration all have a major impact on the economy.

I am running for the presidency because I have a deep love for our country and because I believe that we can do better. I have a simple, clear, bold plan to move our country forward and to take on the really tough issues that many of our leaders have left behind. My plan will require sacrifice from every American citizen in order to build a more perfect union. The result of that sacrifice and hard work will be something that we can all be proud of.

We have a history of doing great things as a nation. It is my opinion that our current generation has the opportunity to stand up, be counted, and do some great things to move our country forward.

One of my favorite quotes is from anthropologist Margaret Mead who said, "Never doubt that a small group of thoughtful, committed citizens can change the world; indeed, it's the only thing that ever has."

Thank you for reading this book. If you have any comments, you can reach me at john@presidentialplaybook.com. ✓

About the Author

John Burke began working at Trek Bicycle in 1984 and has been president of the company since 1997. During his tenure, Trek has grown to become one of world's preeminent bicycle brands ridden by cyclists around the world. In addition to leading Trek, John served as chairman of President George W. Bush's President's Council on Physical Fitness and Sports and is a founding member of PeopleForBikes. John is an avid cyclist, passionate sustainability advocate, runner, and a published author. His first book, *One Last Great Thing*, chronicles the life and lessons of John's late father and Trek Bicycle founder, Richard Burke. His second book, *12 Simple Solutions to Save America*, strips partisan spin from twelve pressing issues facing the United States, exposing the facts and potential nonpartisan solutions to each. In his most recent book, *Presidential Playbook 2020: 16 Nonpartisan Solutions to Save America*, Burke provides updated insight to *12 Simple Solutions* with new data and perspectives. John and his wife, Tania, live in Madison, Wisconsin. ●

Endnotes

Introduction

1 David McCullough, speech to Marquette University graduates, 2011

2 John Burke, "12 Simple Solutions to Save America," published by Little Creek Press, June 15, 2016

3 John Gramlich and Kat Devlin, "More people around the world see U.S. power and influence as a 'major threat' to their country," Pew Research Center, Feb. 14, 2019 https://www.pewresearch.org/fact-tank/2019/02/14/more-people-around-the-world-see-u-s-power-and-influence-as-a-major-threat-to-their-country/

4 Julie Ray, "World's Approval of U.S. Leadership Drops to New Low," Gallup, Jan. 18, 2018 https://news.gallup.com/poll/225761/world-approval-leadership-drops-new-low.aspx

5 Robert Penn Warren, "All The King's Men," published in 1946, winner of Pulitzer Prize for Fiction in 1947

6 "The Debt to the Penny and Who Holds It," U.S. Department of the Treasury, updated daily https://www.treasurydirect.gov/NP/debt/current

7 Dylan Matthews, "The myth of the 70,000-page federal tax code," Vox, March 29, 2017 https://www.vox.com/policy-and-politics/2017/3/29/15109214/tax-code-page-count-complexity-simplification-reform-ways-means

8 "NASA, NOAA Analyses Reveal 2019 Second Warmest Year on Record," National Aeronautics and Space Administration, Jan. 15, 2020 https://www.nasa.gov/press-release/nasa-noaa-analyses-reveal-2019-second-warmest-year-on-record

9 "Congress and the Public," Gallup, https://news.gallup.com/poll/1600/congress-public.aspx

10 Daniel Patrick Moynihan, origin of the quote is unclear, as discussed in this article by Lindsey Bever, "This GOP senator just attributed a well-known liberal quote to Ronald Reagan," *The Washington Post*, March 15, 2017 https://www.washingtonpost.com/news/the-fix/wp/2017/03/15/this-gop-senator-just-attributed-a-well-known-liberal-quote-to-ronald-reagan/

11 Ben Sasse, *CNN* interview, July 2, 2017 https://www.facebook.com/cnn/videos/10156969958531509/?v=10156969958531509

12 John F. Kennedy, "New Frontier Speech" upon acceptance of Democratic nomination for president, July 15, 1960 available at The American Presidency Project https://www.presidency.ucsb.edu/documents/address-senator-john-f-kennedy-accepting-the-democratic-party-nomination-for-the with video available from the John F. Kennedy Presidential Library from CBS News https://www.jfklibrary.org/learn/about-jfk/historic-speeches/acceptance-of-democratic-nomination-for-president

13 "World military expenditure grows to $1.8 trillion in 2018," Stockholm International Peace Research Institute, April 20, 2019 https://www.sipri.org/media/press-release/2019/world-military-expenditure-grows-18-trillion-2018

14 "What is the Highway Trust Fund and how is it financed?" Tax Policy Center Urban Institute and Brookings Institution, 2020 https://www.taxpolicycenter.org/briefing-book/what-highway-trust-fund-and-how-it-financed

15 Party Affiliation," Gallup https://news.gallup.com/poll/15370/party-affiliation.aspx

16 Dwight D. Eisenhower, quoted in numerous places including by David Brooks, "The Road to Character," published by Random House, Sept. 13, 2016

17 Celestine Bohlen, "American Democracy is Drowning in Money," *The New York Times*, Sept. 20, 2017 https://www.nytimes.com/ 2017/09/20/opinion/democracy-drowning-cash.html

Core Beliefs

1 Shane Harris, Greg Miller, Josh Dawsey and Ellen Nakashima, "U.S. intelligence reports from January and February warned about a likely pandemic," *The Washington Post*, March 20, 2020 https://www.washingtonpost.com/national-security/us-intelligence-reports-from-january-and-february-warned-about-a-likely-pandemic/2020/03/20/299d8cda-6ad5-11ea-b5f1-a5a804158597_story.html

2 Washington State 2019-nCoV Case Investigation Team led by Michelle L. Holschue, M.P.H., "First Case of 2019 Novel Coronavirus in the United States," *The New England Journal of Medicine*, March 5, 2020 https://www.nejm.org/doi/full/10.1056/NEJMoa2001191

3 David Leonhardt "A Complete List of Trump's Attempts to Play Down Coronavirus," *The New York Times*, March 20, 2020 https://www.nytimes.com/2020/03/15/opinion/trump-coronavirus.html

4 Daniel B. Jernigan, M.D. and the CDC COVID-19 Response Team, "Update Public Health Response to the 2019 Coronavirus Outbreak – United States, February 24, 2020," Centers for Disease Control and Prevention, Feb. 25, 2020 https://www.cdc.gov/mmwr/volumes/69/wr/mm6908e1.htm

5 Aaron Blake, "A Timeline of Trump playing down the coronavirus threat," *The Washington Post*, March 17, 2020 https://www.washingtonpost.com/politics/2020/03/12/trump-coronavirus-timeline

6 Meg Wagner, Joshua Berlinger, Jessie Yeung, Adam Renton and Sheena McKenzie, "March 10 coronavirus news," *CNN News*, March 10, 2020 https://www.cnn.com/world/live-news/coronavirus-outbreak-03-10-20-intl-hnk/index.html

7   Aaron Blake, "A Timeline of Trump playing down the coronavirus threat,"
    The Washington Post, March 17, 2020 https://www.washingtonpost.com/
    politics/2020/03/12/trump-coronavirus-timeline

8   There are numerous stories about the turnaround, including these: Alyson
    Shontell, "The Amazing Story of How Steve Jobs Took Apple From Near
    Bankruptcy to Billions in 13 Years," *Business Insider*, Jan. 19, 2011 https://www.
    businessinsider.com/how-steve-jobs-took-apple-from-near-bankruptcy-to-
    billions-in-13-years-2011-1, and Carmine Gallo, "Steve Jobs Asked One Profound
    Question That Took Apple From Near Bankruptcy to $1 Trillion," *Forbes*, Aug.
    5, 2018 https://www.forbes.com/sites/carminegallo/2018/08/05/steve-jobs-
    asked-one-profound-question-that-took-apple-from-near-bankruptcy-to-1-
    trillion/#168de1329c2f

9   John F. Kennedy, Inaugural Address, Jan. 20, 1961, available via John F. Kennedy
    Presidential Library and Museum https://www.jfklibrary.org/asset-viewer/
    archives/JFKPOF/034/JFKPOF-034-002

10 Abraham Lincoln, Gettysburg Address, delivered on Nov. 19, 1863, transcript
    available at *PBS*, "The Civil War" https://www.pbs.org/kenburns/civil-war/war/
    historical-documents/gettysburg-address/

11 "Over-regulated America," *The Economist*, Feb. 18, 2012 https://www.economist.
    com/leaders/2012/02/18/over-regulated-america

12 Compiled from annual reports by the General Accounting Office issued since
    2011, including this: "Duplication and Cost Saving," General Accounting Office,
    May 21, 2019 https://www.gao.gov/duplication-cost-saving

13 Dylan Matthews, "The myth of the 70,000-page federal tax code," Vox, March
    29, 2017 https://www.vox.com/policy-and-politics/2017/3/29/15109214/tax-code-
    page-count-complexity-simplification-reform-ways-means

14 Steve Jobs, quoted in numerous publications, including this: Walter Isaacson,
    "How Steve Jobs' Love of Simplicity Fueled a Design Revolution," *Smithsonian
    Magazine*, September 2012 https://www.smithsonianmag.com/arts-culture/how-
    steve-jobs-love-of-simplicity-fueled-a-design-revolution-23868877/

16 Nonpartisan Solutions

1   Great Place to Work Institute https://www.greatplacetowork.com/

2   John Cook, Naomi Oreskes, Peter T. Doran, William R.L. Anderegg, Bart
    Verheggen, Ed W. Maibach, J. Stuart Carlton, Stephan Lewandowsky,
    Andrew G. Skuce, Sarah A. Green, "Consensus on Consensus: A Synthesis of
    Consensus Estimates on Human-Caused Global Warming," *Environmental
    Research Letters*, Vol. 11, No. 4, April 13, 2016 https://iopscience.iop.org/
    article/10.1088/1748-9326/11/4/048002

3 Kelsey Reichmann, "Here's how many nuclear warheads exist, and which countries own them," *Defense News*, June 16, 2019 https://www.defensenews.com/global/2019/06/16/heres-how-many-nuclear-warheads-exist-and-which-countries-own-them/

4 "Projected Costs of U.S. Nuclear Forces, 2019-2028," Congressional Budget Office, January 2019 https://www.cbo.gov/system/files/2019-01/54914-NuclearForces.pdf

5 "CMS Office of the Actuary Releases 2018 National Health Expenditures," Office of the Actuary at the Centers for Medicare and Medicaid Services, Dec. 5, 2019 https://www.cms.gov/newsroom/press-releases/cms-office-actuary-releases-2018-national-health-expenditures and Lee J. Miller and Wei Lu, "These Are the Economies With the Most (and Least) Efficient Health Care," *Bloomberg News*, Sept. 19, 2018 https://www.bloomberg.com/news/articles/2018-09-19/u-s-near-bottom-of-health-index-hong-kong-and-singapore-at-top?sref=zcBXJvHi

6 "America's Infrastructure Report Card 2017|GPA: D+" American Society of Civil Engineers https://www.infrastructurereportcard.org/

7 "An Unhappy Anniversary: Federal Gas Tax Reaches 25 years of Stagnation," Institute on Taxation and Economic Policy, Sept. 25, 2018 https://itep.org/an-unhappy-anniversary-federal-gas-tax-reaches-25-years-of-stagnation/ and InflationData.com https://inflationdata.com/Inflation/Inflation_Calculators/Cumulative_Inflation_Calculator.aspx

8 "18.0% Poverty, Under 18 years old in United States," American Community Survey, U.S. Census Bureau, 2018 https://data.census.gov/cedsci/all?q=child%20poverty%20nationwide%20in%202018&hidePreview=false&tid=ACSST1Y2018.S1701&t=Poverty&y=2018; and "How Many Kids in the United States are Living in Poverty?" The Annie E. Casey Foundation, Jan. 21, 2020 https://www.aecf.org/blog/children-living-in-poverty-in-america/#:~:text=In%202018%2C%20a%20family%20of%20two%20adults%20and%20two%20kids,the%20KIDS%20COUNT%20Data%20Center

9 Mieke Eoyang and Matt Bennett, Third Way, "Preserving Security by Curbing Pentagon Spending," *The Hill* blogs, Dec. 13, 2012https://thehill.com/blogs/congress-blog/economy-a-budget/272573-preserving-security-by-curbing-pentagon-spending

10 Fiscal Year 2021 Budget Request Overview, Office of the Under Secretary of Defense, February 2020 https://comptroller.defense.gov/Portals/45/Documents/defbudget/fy2021/fy2021_Budget_Request_Overview_Book.pdf, chapter 1, page 3 and chapter 6, page 1; "VA 2021 Budget Request: Fast Facts, Department of Veterans Affairs, https://www.va.gov/budget/docs/summary/fy2021VAsBudgetFastFacts.pdf; "FY 2021 Budget in Brief," Department of Homeland Security https://www.dhs.gov/sites/default/files/publications/

fy_2021_dhs_bib_web_version.pdf; "Overview of FY 2020 Appropriations for Commerce, Justice, Science and Related Agencies," Congressional Research Service, Jan. 29, 2020 https://fas.org/sgp/crs/misc/R45702.pdf; and "FY 2021 Presidential Budget for NNSA Released," National Nuclear Security Administration, Feb. 10, 2020 https://www.energy.gov/nnsa/articles/fy-2021-presidential-budget-nnsa-released

11 Pew Research Center FactTank, Aug. 16, 2019 https://www.pewresearch.org/fact-tank/2019/08/16/what-the-data-says-about-gun-deaths-in-the-u-s/ and "Everytown for Gun Safety Releases New Report on Gun Violence in America as Gun Violence Survivors Week Begins," Everytown for Gun Safety, Feb. 1, 2019 https://everytown.org/press/everytown-for-gun-safety-releases-new-report-on-gun-violence-in-america-as-gun-violence-survivors-week-begins/

12 "Trends in U.S. Corrections," The Sentencing Project, June 2019 https://www.sentencingproject.org/wp-content/uploads/2016/01/Trends-in-US-Corrections.pdf and Bureau of Justice Statistics Bulletin, Prisoners 1925-81, published December 1982 https://www.bjs.gov/content/pub/pdf/p2581.pdf

13 "Trends in U.S. Corrections," The Sentencing Project, June 2019 https://www.sentencingproject.org/wp-content/uploads/2016/01/Trends-in-US-Corrections.pdf and "World Prison Brief, United Kingdom—England and Wales," Institute for Crime and Justice Policy Research and Birkbeck University of London https://www.prisonstudies.org/country/united-kingdom-england-wales

14 Ronald Reagan, statement on immigration, July 31, 1981, transcript available via *The New York Times* https://www.nytimes.com/1981/07/31/us/reagan-s-statement-on-immigration.html

Solution 1: Demand a High-Performance Government

1   Jim Collins, "Good to Great: Why Some Companies Make the Leap … and Others Don't," published by Harper Business, July 19, 2011

2   "Coronavirus Live Updates: Trump Warns of 'Very, Very Painful Two Weeks' Ahead," *The New York Times*, March 31, 2020 https://www.nytimes.com/2020/03/31/world/coronavirus-live-news-updates.html

3   Elisabeth Buchwald, "What we can learn from South Korea and Singapore's efforts to stop coronavirus (besides wearing face masks)," *MarketWatch*, March 31, 2020 https://www.marketwatch.com/story/what-we-can-learn-from-south-korea-and-singapores-efforts-to-stop-coronavirus-in-addition-to-wearing-face-masks-2020-03-31

4   "Coronavirus Live Updates: Trump Warns of 'Very, Very Painful Two Weeks' Ahead," *The New York Times*, March 31, 2020 https://www.nytimes.com/2020/03/31/world/coronavirus-live-news-updates.html

5   Hyonhee Shin and Cynthia Kim, "South Korea to boost dollar supply to ease economic pressures," Reuters, March 17, 2020 https://www.reuters.com/article/us-health-coronavirus-southkorea-toll/south-korea-to-boost-dollar-supply-to-ease-economic-pressures-idUSKBN215054

6   Lawrence Delevingne and Howard Schneider "U.S. stimulus package is biggest ever, but may not be big enough," *Reuters News Service*, March 30, 2020 https://www.reuters.com/article/us-health-coronavirus-fed-stimulus-analy/us-stimulus-package-is-biggest-ever-but-may-not-be-big-enough-idUSKBN21H0E7

7   Robert Samuelson, "Why we don't prepare for the future," *The Washington Post*, Sept. 9, 2018 https://www.washingtonpost.com/opinions/why-we-dont-prepare-for-the-future/2018/09/09/cb91cc34-b2c3-11e8-aed9-001309990777_story.html

8   Dennis Cauchon, "Some Federal Workers More Likely to Die Than Lose Jobs," USA Today, July 19, 2011 https://usatoday30.usatoday.com/ news/washington/2011-07-18-fderal-job-security_n.html

9   Angie Drobnic Holan, "Firing federal workers is difficult," Politifact.com, Poynter Institute, Sept. 5, 2007 https://www.politifact.com/article/2007/sep/05/mcainfederal/

10 Pres. Franklin D. Roosevelt, letter, Aug. 16, 1937, The American Presidency Project https://www.presidency.ucsb.edu/documents/ letter-the-resolution-federation-federal-employees-against-strikes-federalservice

11 "Captive Politicians," *The New York Times*, July 9, 1975 https:// www.nytimes.com/1975/07/09/archives/captive-politicians.html

12 Andrew J. Coulson, "A Less Perfect Union," The American Spectator, June 17, 2011, available via Cato Institute https://www.cato. org/publications/commentary/less-perfect-union

13 "Public Sector Unions: Top Contributors to Federal Candidates, Parties and Outside Groups," OpenSecrets.org, Center for Responsive Politics https://www.opensecrets.org/ industries./contrib.php?cycle=2020&ind=P04

14 Quoted in Jay P. Greene, "Steve Jobs on Education," Education Next, Oct. 6, 2011 https://www.educationnext.org/steve-jobs-oneducation/

15 Quoted in Gregg Keizer, "Jobs Bashes Teachers Unions," PCWorld, Feb. 20, 2007 https://www.pcworld.com/ article/129214/article.html

16 John Doerr, "Measure What Matters," publisher Generic, Jan. 1, 2018 S

17 John Doerr, "Measure What Matters," publisher Generic, Jan. 1, 2018 S

18 John Doerr, "Measure What Matters," publisher Generic, Jan. 1, 2018 S

Solution 2: Initiate Climate Change Leadership FAST!

1   Quoted in Aiko Stevenson, HuffPost, March 1, 2012 https://www.
    huffpost.com/entry/robert-swan-antarctica_b_1315047?guccounter=1&
    guce_referrer=aHR0cHM6Ly93d3cuZ29vZ2xlLmNvbS8&guce_referrer_
    sig=AQAAADKhgGY8vix9C8IIU_4_QvT4R3cqGyvGJGXSHMsxOO45zDzSk5X
    6s-jbIV4YQ-ukL_m9HMWuweugrT87jW5ZEEZjEnQwm3U3JulqJnelTDpA3JGOQ
    9oaOoAI6KUsseRGDO3XpANW8jGvOwwr0A9cWMtZbEVovrGZFc71h-qU2ZFy

2   John Cook, Naomi Oreskes, Peter T. Doran, William R.L. Anderegg, Bart
    Verheggen, Ed W. Maibach, J. Stuart Carlton, Stephan Lewandowsky,
    Andrew G. Skuce, Sarah A. Green, "Consensus on Consensus: A Synthesis of
    Consensus Estimates on Human-Caused Global Warming," Environmental
    Research Letters, Vol. 11, No. 4, April 13, 2016 https://iopscience.iop.org/
    article/10.1088/1748-9326/11/4/048002

3   Thomas Friedman, Thank you for Being Late: An Optimist's Guide to Thriving in
    the Age of Accelerations, published by Farrar, Straus and Giroux, Nov. 22, 2016

4   Carbon dioxide levels in atmosphere hit record high in May," Science Daily, June
    4, 2019 https://www.sciencedaily.com/releases/2019/06/190604140109.htm

5   National Aeronautics and Space Administration (NASA) and the National
    Oceanic and Atmospheric Administration (NOAA), Jan. 15, 2020 https://www.
    nasa.gov/press-release/nasa-noaa-analyses-reveal-2019-second-warmest-year-
    on-record

6   NOAA's National Centers for Environmental Information Global Climate Report—
    Annual 2019, January 2020 https://www.ncdc.noaa.gov/sotc/global/201913

7   Climate change and human health," World Health Organization, 2020
    https://www.who.int/globalchange/summary/en/index5.html

8   World Wildlife Fund, "WWF Report Reveals Staggering Extent of Human Impact
    on Planet," Oct. 29, 2018 https://www.worldwildlife.org/press-releases/wwf-
    report-reveals-staggering-extent-of-human-impact-on-planet

9   U.S. Global Change Research Program https://www.globalchange.gov/browse/
    indicators/global-sea-level-rise

10 Maggie Gordon, "Repeat Flooding has Residents Asking: Is Houston Worth
    It?" Houston Chronicle, Sept. 23, 2019 https://www.houstonchronicle.com/
    news/houston-texas/houston/article/Repeat-flooding-has-residents-asking-Is-
    Houston-14456965.php

11 Phillip Reese, The Sacramento Bee, "California wildfires in 2017: A staggering toll
    of lost life and homes" Dec. 31, 2017 https://www.sacbee.com/news/california/
    fires/article192402749.html; and Wikipediahttps://en.wikipedia.org/wiki/2017_
    California_wildfires

12 Dennis Romero, "California had nation's worst fire season in 2018," NBC News, March 9, 2019 https://www.nbcnews.com/news/us-news/california-had-nation-s-worst-fire-season-2018-n981431

13 California Department of Forestry and Fire Protection, "Top 20 Largest California Wildfires" Aug. 8, 2019 https://www.fire.ca.gov/media/5510/top20_acres.pdf

14 "Assessing the U.S. Climate in 2017: 2017 was the Third Warmest Year on Record," NOAA's National Centers for Environmental Information, Jan. 5, 2018 https://www.ncei.noaa.gov/news/national-climate-201712

15 Brad Plumer, "U.S. Carbon Emissions Surged in 2018 Even as Coal Plants Closed," *The New York Times*, Jan. 8, 2019 https://www.nytimes.com/2019/01/08/climate/greenhouse-gas-emissions-increase.html

16 "List of countries by carbon dioxide emissions," Wikipedia https://en.wikipedia.org/wiki/List_of_countries_by_carbon_dioxide_emissions, from EDGAR database created by the European Commission and Netherlands Environmental Assessment Agency, released in 2018

17 Alister Doyle, "Weather extremes, fossil fuel pollution cost US $240 billion: study," Reuters News, Sept. 27, 2017 https://www.reuters.com/article/us-climatechange-usa/weather-extremes-fossil-fuel-pollution-cost-us-240-billion-study-idUSKCN1C22AM

18 "Growing at a slower pace, world population is expected to reach 9.7 billion in 2050 and could peak at nearly 11 billion around 2100," United Nations Department of Economic and Social Affairs, June 17, 2019 https://www.un.org/development/desa/en/news/population/world-population-prospects-2019.html

19 Thomas L. Friedman, "Thank You for Being Late: An Optimist's Guide to Thriving in the Age of Accelerations," published by Farrar, Straus and Giroux, Nov. 22, 2016

20 Benjamin Storrow, "Global CO_2 Emissions Rise After Paris Climate Agreement Signed," Scientific American, March 24, 2018 https://www.scientificamerican.com/article/global-co2-emissions-rise-after-paris-climate-agreement-signed/

21 Matthew Green, "Growth in global carbon emissions slowed in 2019: report," Reuters News, Dec. 3, 2019 https://www.reuters.com/article/us-climate-change-accord-carbon/growth-in-global-carbon-emissions-slowed-in-2019-report-idUSKBN1Y800W

22 Rebecca Hersher, "U.S. Formally Begins to Leave the Paris Climate Agreement," National Public Radio, Nov. 4, 2019 https://www.npr.org/2019/11/04/773474657/u-s-formally-begins-to-leave-the-paris-climate-agreement

23 David Hasemyer, "U.S. Soldiers Falling Ill, Dying in the Heat as Climate Warms," Inside Climate News and NBC News, July 23, 2019 https://insideclimatenews.org/news/23072019/military-heat-death-illness-climate-change-risk-security-global-warming-benning-bragg-chaffee

24 Henry Fountain, "Researchers Link Syrian Conflict to a Drought Made Worse by Climate Change," *The New York Times*, March 2, 2015 https://www.nytimes.com/2015/03/03/science/earth/study-links-syria-conflict-to-drought-caused-by-climate-change.html. Syria, Events of 2018," Human Rights Watch World Report 2019 https://www.hrw.org/world-report/2019/country-chapters/syria; and Colin P. Kelley, Shahrzad Mohtadi, Mark A. Cane, Richard Seager and Yochanan Kushnir, "Climate change in the Fertile Crescent and implications of the recent Syrian drought," National Academy of Sciences, March 17, 2015 https://www.jstor.org/stable/26462026?mag=climate-change-and-syrias-civil-war&seq=1#metadata_info_tab_contents

25 Antonio Guterres, "Secretary—General's remarks at the opening of the COP 24," United Nations Secretary-General, Dec. 3, 2018 https://www.un.org/sg/en/content/sg/statement/2018-12-03/secretary-generals-remarks-opening-cop-24

26 Antonio Guterres, "Secretary-General Antonio Guterres Calls for Climate Leadership, Outlines Expectations for Next Three Years," United Nations, Climate Change, Sept. 11, 2018 https://unfccc.int/news/un-secretary-general-antonio-guterres-calls-for-climate-leadership-outlines-expectations-for-next

27 John Schwartz, "'A Conservative Climate Solution': Republican Group Calls for Carbon Tax," *The New York Times*, Feb. 7, 2017 https://www.nytimes.com/2017/02/07/science/a-conservative-climate-solution-republican-group-calls-for-carbon-tax.html

28 Al Gore, "Al Gore: The Climate Crisis is the Battle of our Time, and We Can Win," *The New York Times*, Sept. 20, 2019 https://www.nytimes.com/2019/09/20/opinion/al-gore-climate-change.html

Solution 3: Reduce the Risk of Nuclear War

1 Noam Chomsky, "Cuban missile crisis: how the U.S. played Russian roulette with nuclear war," The Guardian, Oct. 15, 2012 https://www.theguardian.com/commentisfree/2012/oct/15/cuban-missile-crisis-russian-roulette

2 Ashley Lutz, "This chart shows the terrifying power of modern nuclear bombs," Business Insider, June 19, 2012 https://www.businessinsider.com/this-chart-shows-the-terrifying-power-of-modern-nuclear-bombs-2012-6

3 Gayle Spinazze, "Press Release—It is now 100 seconds to Midnight," Bulletin of the Atomic Scientists, Jan. 23, 2020 https://thebulletin.org/2020/01/press-release-it-is-now-100-seconds-to-midnight/#

4   Quoted and cited in Walter Isaacson, "Einstein: His Life and Universe," published by Simon & Schuster, 2007. Original source is an interview with Alfred Werner, Liberal Judiasm, April-May 1945

5   Ed Pilkington, "U.S. nearly detonated atomic bomb over North Carolina—secret document," The Guardian, Sept. 20, 2013 https://www.theguardian.com/world/2013/sep/20/usaf-atomic-bomb-north-carolina-1961

6   Michael Dobbs, "The Real Story of the 'Football' That Follows the President Everywhere," Smithsonian Magazine, October 2014 https://www.smithsonianmag.com/history/real-story-football-follows-president-everywhere-180952779/

7   "The 3 a.m. phone call," The National Security Archive, George Washington University, quoting from Robert M. Gates, "From the Shadows: The Ultimate Insider's Story of Five Presidents and How They Won the Cold War," Simon & Schuster, 2007 https://nsarchive2.gwu.edu/nukevault/ebb371/

8   Martin E. Hellman, "On the Probability of Nuclear War," Stanford University Electrical Engineering website https://ee.stanford.edu/~hellman/opinion/inevitability.html Originally an op-ed, "Arms race can only lead to one end: If we don't change our thinking, someone will drop the big one," Houston Post, April 4, 1985.

9   Martin E. Hellman, "On the Probability of Nuclear War," Stanford University Electrical Engineering website https://ee.stanford.edu/~hellman/opinion/inevitability.html Originally an op-ed, "Arms race can only lead to one end: If we don't change our thinking, someone will drop the big one," Houston Post, April 4, 1985.

10 Martin E. Hellman, "On the Probability of Nuclear War," Stanford University Electrical Engineering website https://ee.stanford.edu/~hellman/opinion/inevitability.html Originally an op-ed, "Arms race can only lead to one end: If we don't change our thinking, someone will drop the big one," Houston Post, April 4, 1985.

11 Kelsey Reichmann, "Here's how many nuclear warheads exist, and which countries own them," Defense News, June 16, 2019 https://www.defensenews.com/global/2019/06/16/heres-how-many-nuclear-warheads-exist-and-which-countries-own-them/

12 Jo Craven McGinty, "About Those Nuclear Codes: How Do They Work?" The Wall Street Journal, Sept. 22, 2017 https://www.wsj.com/articles/nuclear-codes-are-rarely-far-from-the-presidents-side-1506085202

13 "50 Facts About U.S. Nuclear Weapons Today," Brookings Institution, April 28, 2014 https://www.brookings.edu/research/50-facts-about-u-s-nuclear-weapons-today/; and Loren Thompson, "Navy's D5 Missile, Most Powerful U.S. Weapon, to Provide Backbone of Nuclear Deterrent Through 2040," *Forbes*, June 5, 2017 https://www.forbes.com/sites/lorenthompson/2017/06/05/navys-d5-missile-most-powerful-u-s-weapon-to-provide-backbone-of-nuclear-deterrent-through-2040/#73f7d2cd72e6

14 Martin Hellman, "Nuclear War: Inevitable or Preventable?" in "Breakthrough: Emerging New Thinking," published by Walker & Co., Feb. 1, 1988; chapter available at https://ee.stanford.edu/~hellman/Breakthrough/book/chapters/hellman.html

15 Kelsey Reichmann, "Here's how many nuclear warheads exist, and which countries own them," Defense News, June 16, 2019 https://www.defensenews.com/global/2019/06/16/heres-how-many-nuclear-warheads-exist-and-which-countries-own-them/

16 Defense News, June 16, 2019 https://www.defensenews.com/global/2019/06/16/heres-how-many-nuclear-warheads-exist-and-which-countries-own-them/

17 Martin Hellman, "Nuclear War: Inevitable or Preventable?" in "Breakthrough: Emerging New Thinking," published by Walker & Co., Feb. 1, 1988; chapter available at https://ee.stanford.edu/~hellman/Breakthrough/book/chapters/hellman.html

18 Martin Hellman, "How Risky is Nuclear Optimism?" Bulletin of the Atomic Scientists, 2011 https://ee.stanford.edu/~hellman/publications/75.pdf

19 Projected Costs of U.S. Nuclear Forces, 2019-2028," Congressional Budget Office, January 2019 https://www.cbo.gov/system/files/2019-01/54914-NuclearForces.pdf

20 Dan Farber, "Nuclear Attack a Ticking Time Bomb, Experts Warn, CBS News, May 4, 2010 https://www.cbsnews.com/news/nuclear-attack-a-ticking-time-bomb-experts-warn/

21 Jaime Fuller and Chas Danner, "At Least 129 Dead After Explosions and Shootings in Paris," New York Magazine Intelligencer, Nov. 14, 2015 https://nymag.com/intelligencer/2015/11/many-dead-after-explosion-shootings-in-paris.html

22 September 11 Attacks," History.com editors, originally written Aug. 25, 2018; updated Sept. 11, 2019 https://www.history.com/topics/21st-century/9-11-attacks

23 Max Bergmann, "Colin Powell: Nuclear Weapons are useless," Think Progress, Jan. 27, 2010 reporting on Powell's introduction to the 2010 documentary "Nuclear Tipping Point" produced by Nuclear Threat Initiative https://thinkprogress.org/colin-powell-nuclear-weapons-are-useless-4ab6657759c7/

24 "Nuclear Tipping Point," produced by Nuclear Threat Initiative, 2010, video available at https://www.nti.org/about/projects/nuclear-tipping-point/; Cited in sources including Martin E. Hellman, "How Risky is Nuclear Optimism," Bulletin of the Atomic Scientists, Oct. 13, 2016 https://journals.sagepub.com/doi/full/10.1177/0096340211399873

25 Gary Schaub, Jr. and James Forsyth, Jr., "An Arsenal We Can All Live With," *The New York Times*, May 23, 2010 https://www.nytimes.com/2010/05/24/opinion/24schaub.html

26 "Nuclear Darkness, Global Climate Change and Nuclear Darkness—The Deadly Consequences of Nuclear War," https://www.nucleardarkness.org/solutions/eliminatehighalertnuclearweapons/; U.N. Resolution 62/36, "Decreasing the operational readiness of nuclear weapons systems" https://undocs.org/en/A/RES/62/36

27 Matthew Bunn, "Securing the Bomb 2010 — Securing All Nuclear Materials in Four Years," page 69, Project on Managing the Atom, Belfer Center for Science and International Affairs, Harvard University, April 2010 https://scholar.harvard.edu/files/matthew_bunn/files/securing_the_bomb_2010.pdf

28 President John F. Kennedy, "Address Before the General Assembly of the United Nations," Sept. 25, 1961, accessible via John F. Kennedy Presidential Library and Museum https://www.jfklibrary.org/archives/other-resources/john-f-kennedy-speeches/united-nations-19610925

Solution 4: Fix the Health Care System

1   Jack LaLanne, available via sources including AZ Quotes, https://www.azquotes.com/quote/543521

2   "CMS Office of the Actuary Releases 2018 National Health Expenditures," Office of the Actuary at the Centers for Medicare and Medicaid Services, Dec. 5, 2019 https://www.cms.gov/newsroom/press-releases/cms-office-actuary-releases-2018-national-health-expenditures

3   "Health spending," Organization for Economic Cooperation and Development, 2020 https://data.oecd.org/healthres/health-spending.htm

4   Lee J. Miller and Wei Lu, "These Are the Economies With the Most (and Least) Efficient Health Care," *Bloomberg News*, Sept. 19, 2018 https://www.bloomberg.com/news/articles/2018-09-19/u-s-near-bottom-of-health-index-hong-kong-and-singapore-at-top?sref=zcBXJvHi

5   Lee J. Miller and Wei Lu, "These Are the Economies With the Most (and Least) Efficient Health Care," *Bloomberg News*, Sept. 19, 2018 https://www.bloomberg.com/news/articles/2018-09-19/u-s-near-bottom-of-health-index-hong-kong-and-singapore-at-top?sref=zcBXJvHi

6   —Kate Knibbs, "The Race to Keep Health Care Workers Protected from Covid-19," *Wired*, March 27, 2020 https://www.wired.com/story/coronavirus-covid-19-healthcare-risks-equipment/

7   Lee J. Miller and Wei Lu, "These Are the Economies With the Most (and Least) Efficient Health Care," *Bloomberg News*, Sept. 19, 2018 https://www.bloomberg.com/news/articles/2018-09-19/u-s-near-bottom-of-health-index-hong-kong-and-singapore-at-top?sref=zcBXJvHi

8   Sources for the Canadian information: World Health Rankings https://www.worldlifeexpectancy.com/canada-life-expectancy#:~:text=Canada%20%3A%20Life%20Expectancy&text=According%20to%20the%20latest%20WHO,Life%20Expectancy%20ranking%20of%207.; Jason Miller, "Canadian spending on health care expected to increase by 4.2 percent over last year, report says," The Star, Nov. 20, 2018 https://www.thestar.com/news/canada/2018/11/20/canadian-spending-on-health-care-expected-to-increase-by-42-per-cent-over-last-year-report-says.html; and "National Health Expenditure Trends, 1975 to 2019, Canadian Institute for Health Information https://www.cihi.ca/en/national-health-expenditure-trends-1975-to-2019

9   Uptin Saiidi, "U.S. life expectancy has been declining. Here's why," CNBC News, July 9, 2019 https://www.cnbc.com/2019/07/09/us-life-expectancy-has-been-declining-heres-why.html

10 Barack Obama, Remarks at the White House Health Care Forum, March 5, 2009, available via *The New York Times* https://www.nytimes.com/2009/03/05/us/politics/05obama-text.html

11 Chris Strauss, "Gary Player blasts America's 'tsunami of obesity,'" For The Win, *USA Today* Sports, July 9, 2013 https://ftw.usatoday.com/2013/07/gary-player-blasts-americas-obesity-problem

12 NHE Fact Sheet, Centers for Medicare and Medicaid Services, Dec. 5, 2019 https://www.cms.gov/Research-Statistics-Data-and-Systems/Statistics-Trends-and-Reports/NationalHealthExpendData/NHE-Fact-Sheet and Matej Mikulic, "Health expenditure as a percentage of gross domestic product in selected countries in 2018," Statista.com, Nov. 12, 2019 https://www.statista.com/statistics/268826/health-expenditure-as-gdp-percentage-in-oecd-countries/

13 Sally C. Pipes, "Medicare at 50: Hello, Mid-Life Crisis," *The Wall Street Journal*—Opinion, July 29, 2015 https://www.wsj.com/articles/medicare-at-50-hello-mid-life-crisis-1438211061https://www.wsj.com/articles/medicare-at-50-hello-mid-life-crisis-1438211061

14 Atul Gawande, "Overkill," The New Yorker, May 11, 2015https://www.newyorker.com/magazine/2015/05/11/overkill-atul-gawande

15 Historical data, Centers for Medicare and Medicaid Services, NHE Summary, Table 1 https://www.cms.gov/Research-Statistics-Data-and-Systems/Statistics-Trends-and-Reports/NationalHealthExpendData/NationalHealthAccountsHistorical

16 2019 Employer Health Benefits Survey, Kaiser Family Foundation, Sept. 25, 2019 https://www.kff.org/report-section/ehbs-2019-summary-of-findings/

17 NHE Fact Sheet, Centers for Medicare and Medicaid Services, Dec. 5, 2019 https://www.cms.gov/Research-Statistics-Data-and-Systems/Statistics-Trends-and-Reports/NationalHealthExpendData/NHE-Fact-Sheet

18 NHE Fact Sheet 2018, Centers for Medicare and Medicaid Services, Dec. 5, 2019 https://www.cms.gov/Research-Statistics-Data-and-Systems/Statistics-Trends-and-Reports/NationalHealthExpendData/NHE-Fact-Sheet

19 NHE Fact Sheet, Centers for Medicare and Medicaid Services, Dec. 5, 2019 https://www.cms.gov/Research-Statistics-Data-and-Systems/Statistics-Trends-and-Reports/NationalHealthExpendData/NHE-Fact-Sheet, Table 3, National Health Expenditures by Source of Funds

20 "Surgery 2015-2017 Final Report," National Quality Forum, April 2017 https://www.qualityforum.org/Publications/2017/04/Surgery_2015-2017_Final_Report.aspx

21 Steven Brill, "Bitter Pill: Why Medical Bills Are Killing Us," *TIME* April 4, 2013 https://time.com/198/bitter-pill-why-medical-bills-are-killing-us/

22 Steven Brill, "Bitter Pill: Why Medical Bills Are Killing Us," *TIME* April 4, 2013 https://time.com/198/bitter-pill-why-medical-bills-are-killing-us/

23 Mike Dennison, "Insurance interests total 1/4 of Baucus' fundraising," *Montana Standard*, June 14, 2009

24 Bob Herman, "The sky-high pay of health care CEOs," Axios, July 24, 2017 https://www.axios.com/the-sky-high-pay-of-health-care-ceos-1513303956-d5b874a8-b4a0-4e74-9087-353a2ef1ba83.html

25 Steven Brill, "Bitter Pill: Why Medical Bills Are Killing Us," *TIME*, April 4, 2013 https://time.com/198/bitter-pill-why-medical-bills-are-killing-us/

26 "Body Measurements," Centers for Disease Control and Prevention, National Center for Health Statistics, May 3, 2017 https://www.cdc.gov/nchs/fastats/body-measurements.htm, and "Americans Slightly Taller, Much Heavier Than 40 Years Ago," CDC National Center for Health Statistics, Oct. 27, 2004 https://www.cdc.gov/media/pressrel/r041027.htm; also Christopher Ingraham, "The Average American woman now weighs as much as the average 1960s man," *The Washington Post*, June 12, 2015 https://www.washingtonpost.com/news/wonk/wp/2015/06/12/look-at-how-much-weight-weve-gained-since-the-1960s/

27 "Prevalence of Obesity Among Adults and Youth: United States 2015-2016," Centers for Disease Control and Prevention, National Center for Health Statistics, October 2017 https://www.cdc.gov/nchs/products/databriefs/db288.htm

28 Jane E. Brody, "Half of Us Face Obesity, Dire Projections Show," *The New York Times*, Feb. 10, 2020 https://www.nytimes.com/2020/02/10/well/live/half-of-us-face-obesity-dire-projections-show.html

29 Andrew Jacobs, "Two Top Medical Groups Call for Soda Taxes and Advertising Curbs on Sugary Drinks," *The New York Times*, March 25, 2019 https://www.nytimes.com/2019/03/25/health/soda-taxes-sugary-drinks-advertising.html

30 Nathan Bomey, "Philadelphia soda tax caused 'substantial decline' in soda sales, study finds," *USA Today*, May 15, 2019 https://www.usatoday.com/story/money/2019/05/15/philadelphia-soda-tax-sales-study/3677713002/

31 Janice Hughes and Dennis Hughes, "Interview with Jack LaLanne," Share Guide, publication date unspecified http://www.shareguide.com/LaLanne.html

32 https://gamechangersmovie.com/

33 CMS Fast Facts, Centers for Medicare and Medicaid Services, Dec. 4, 2019 https://www.cms.gov/Research-Statistics-Data-and-Systems/Statistics-Trends-and-Reports/CMS-Fast-Facts

34 Katy Pallister, "Medicare For All Would Save More than 68,000 Lives and $450 Billion Every Year, According to New Study," IFLScience!, Feb. 17, 2020 https://www.iflscience.com/health-and-medicine/medicare-for-all-would-save-more-than-68000-lives-and-450-billion-every-year-according-to-new-study/ and Alison P. Galvani, Alyssa S. Parpia, Eric M. Foster, Burton H. Singer and Meagan C. Fitzpatrick, "Improving the Prognosis of Health Care in the USA," The Lancet, Feb. 15, 2020 https://www.thelancet.com/journals/lancet/article/PIIS0140-6736(19)33019-3/fulltext

35 Elisabeth Rosenthal, "Those Indecipherable Medical Bills? They're One Reason Health Care Costs So Much," *The New York Times* Magazine, March 29, 2017 https://www.nytimes.com/2017/03/29/magazine/those-indecipherable-medical-bills-theyre-one-reason-health-care-costs-so-much.html

36 Bill Gates, "The next outbreak? We're not ready," TED Talks, March 2015 https://www.ted.com/talks/bill_gates_the_next_outbreak_we_re_not_ready?language=en

Solution 5: Rebuild America

1 James M. Perry, *The Wall Street Journal*, Oct. 27, 1995 https://www.fhwa.dot.gov/interstate/quotable.cfm

2 "How High are Other Nations' Gas Taxes?" Tax Foundation, May 2, 2019 https://taxfoundation.org/oecd-gas-tax/

3   "An Unhappy Anniversary: Federal Gas Tax Reaches 25 years of Stagnation,"
    Institute on Taxation and Economic Policy, Sept. 25, 2018 https://itep.org/an-
    unhappy-anniversary-federal-gas-tax-reaches-25-years-of-stagnation/

4   InflationData.com https://inflationdata.com/Inflation/Inflation_Calculators/
    Cumulative_Inflation_Calculator.aspx

5   U.S. Census Bureau (census.gov), https://www.multpl.com/united-states-
    population/table/by-year

6   U.S Department of Transportation Federal Highway Administration
    https://www.fhwa.dot.gov/ohim/summary95/mv200.pdf, Statista.com

7   "Increase Excise Taxes on Motor Fuels and Index for Inflation," Congressional
    Budget Office, Dec. 13, 2018 https://www.cbo.gov/budget-options/2018/54817

8   "America's Infrastructure Report Card 2017|GPA: D+" American Society of Civil
    Engineers https://www.infrastructurereportcard.org/

9   "America's Infrastructure Report Card 2017|GPA: D+" American Society of Civil
    Engineers https://www.infrastructurereportcard.org/

10 Ron Nixon, "Human Cost Rises as Old Bridges, Dams and Roads Go Unrepaired,"
    The New York Times, Nov. 5, 2015 https://www.nytimes.com/2015/11/06/us/
    politics/human-cost-rises-as-old-bridges-dams-and-roads-go-unrepaired.html

11 Federal Highway Administration https://www.fhwa.dot.gov/infrastructure/
    gastax.cfm

12 Tax Foundation https://taxfoundation.org/oecd-gas-tax/, Organization for
    Cooperation and Economic Development

13 Federal Highway Administration https://www.fhwa.dot.gov/highwayhistory/
    reagan_staa_01.cfm

14 "Public Transportation Facts," American Public Transportation Association,
    https://www.apta.com/news-publications/public-transportation-facts/

Solution 6: Increase Opportunity in America

1   President Ronald Reagan, "1981 Inaugural Address," Jan. 20, 1981, audio available
    at the Ronald Reagan Presidential Foundation and Institute https://www.
    reaganfoundation.org/programs-events/webcasts-and-podcasts/podcasts/
    words-to-live-by/1981-inaugural-address/ and written version on Wikipedia at
    https://en.wikisource.org/wiki/Ronald_Reagan%27s_First_Inaugural_Address

2   John Christoffersen, Associated Press, "Rising Inequality 'Most Important
    Problem,' says Nobel-winning economist," St. Louis Post-Dispatch, Oct. 14, 2013
    https://www.stltoday.com/business/local/rising-inequality-most-important-
    problem-says-nobel-winning-economist/article_a5065957-05c3-5ac0-ba5b-
    dab91c22973a.html

3   Peter Grier, "Rich-poor gap gaining attention," The Christian Science Monitor, June 14, 2005 https://www.csmonitor.com/2005/0614/p01s03-usec.html

4   Barack Obama, "Remarks by the President on Economic Mobility," The White House, Office of the Press Secretary, Dec. 4, 2013 https://obamawhitehouse.archives.gov/the-press-office/2013/12/04/remarks-president-economic-mobility

5   Michael E. Porter, Jan W. Rivkin, Mihir A. Desai, with Manjari Raman, "Problems Unsolved and a Nation Divided—The State of U.S. Competitiveness 2016," Harvard Business School, September 2016 https://www.hbs.edu/competitiveness/Documents/problems-unsolved-and-a-nation-divided.pdf

6   John Cassidy, "American Inequality in Six Charts," The New Yorker, Nov. 18, 2013, including data from Thomas Piketty and Emmanuel Saez, University of California, Berkeley https://www.newyorker.com/news/john-cassidy/american-inequality-in-six-charts

7   Emmanuel Saez, Thomas Piketty and Gabriel Zucman, "Economic Growth in the United States: A Tale of Two Countries," Washington Center for Equitable Growth, Dec. 6, 2016 https://equitablegrowth.org/economic-growth-in-the-united-states-a-tale-of-two-countries/

8   Rakesh Kochhar, "The American middle class is stable in size, but losing ground financially to upper income families." Pew Research Center FactTank, Sept. 6, 2018 https://www.pewresearch.org/fact-tank/2018/09/06/the-american-middle-class-is-stable-in-size-but-losing-ground-financially-to-upper-income-families/

9   Jessica Semega, Melissa Kollar, John Creamer and Abinash Mohanty, "Income and Poverty in the United States: 2018," United State Census Bureau, Sept. 17, 2019 https://www.census.gov/library/publications/2019/demo/p60-266.html)

10 "CO2.2: Child Poverty,"Organization for Economic Development, Nov. 2019 https://www.oecd.org/els/CO_2_2_Child_Poverty.pdf

11 Dylan Scott and Alvin Chang, "The Republican tax bill will exacerbate income inequality in America," Vox, Dec. 4, 2017 https://www.vox.com/policy-and-politics/2017/12/2/16720952/senate-tax-bill-inequality

12 Charles M. Blow, "Reducing Our Obscene Level of Child Poverty," *The New York Times*, Jan. 28, 2015 https://www.nytimes.com/2015/01/28/opinion/charles-blow-reducing-our-obscene-level-of-child-poverty.html

13 Earl Warren, U.S. Supreme Court Chief Justice, "Brown v. Board of Education," 1953 accessible via U.S. Library of Congress https://www.loc.gov/item/usrep347483/

14 Alana Semuels, "Good School, Rich School; Bad School, Poor School," *The Atlantic*, Aug. 25, 2016 https://www.theatlantic.com/business/archive/2016/08/property-taxes-and-unequal-schools/497333/

15 Alana Semuels, "Good School, Rich School; Bad School, Poor School," *The Atlantic*, Aug. 25, 2016 https://www.theatlantic.com/business/archive/2016/08/property-taxes-and-unequal-schools/497333/

16 "Update 2020," U.S. Social Security Administration https://www.ssa.gov/pubs/EN-05-10003.pdf

Solution 7: Reform Congress

1 Brad Thor, "Full Black: A Thriller," published by Atria Books, July 26, 2011, sold by Simon and Schuster Digital Sales

2 Congress and the Public," Gallup, https://news.gallup.com/poll/1600/congress-public.aspx

3 U.S. Department of the Treasury, Bureau of the Fiscal Service https://www.treasurydirect.gov/NP/debt/current

4 Jonathan Weisman, "Senate Democrats Offer a Budget, Then the Amendments Fly," *The New York Times*, March 22, 2013 https://www.nytimes.com/2013/03/23/us/politics/senate-democrats-offer-a-budget-then-the-amendments-fly.html

5 Soo Rin Kim, "The price of winning just got higher, especially in the Senate," The Center for Responsive Politics, OpenSecrets.org, Nov. 9, 2016 https://www.opensecrets.org/news/2016/11/the-price-of-winning-just-got-higher-especially-in-the-senate/

6 Karl Evers-Hillstrom, "Democrats ride monster fundraising to take the House, GOP successfully picks its Senate battles," OpenSecrets.org, Nov. 7, 2018 https://www.opensecrets.org/news/2018/11/2018-wrap-up-am/

7 "Congressional Revolving Doors: The Journey from Congress to K Street," Public Citizen's Congress Watch, July 2005 https://www.citizen.org/wp-content/uploads/Congressional-Revolving-Doors-2005.pdf

8 Elliot Gerson, "To Make America Great Again, We Need to Leave the Country," The Atlantic, July 10, 2012 https://www.theatlantic.com/national/archive/2012/07/to-make-america-great-again-we-need-to-leave-the-country/259653/

9 Dan Friedman, "Former Congressmen make huge salaries as lobbyists while still collecting congressional pensions," *New York Daily News*, May 24, 2014 https://www.nydailynews.com/news/politics/congressman-bank-lobbyists-article-1.1804659

10 Nick Penniman, CEO and founder of Issue One, in C-SPAN interview, Jan. 3, 2018 https://www.c-span.org/video/?c4706765/time-spent-fundraising-congress

11 Paul V. Fontelo and David Hawkings, "Ranking the Net Worth of the 115th," Roll Call, November 2019 https://www.rollcall.com/wealth-of-congress

12 "Retirement Benefits for Members of Congress," Congressional Research Service, Aug. 8, 2019 https://crsreports.congress.gov/product/pdf/RL/RL30631

13 "The Book of the States 2017," The Council of State Governments http://knowledgecenter.csg.org/kc/system/files/4.4.2017.pdf

14 "'It looks like gerrymandering,'" Baltimore Sun editorial, March 8, 2018 https://www.baltimoresun.com/opinion/editorial/bs-ed-0312-gerrymandering-20180308-story.html

15 Wallace McKelvey, "Sailboats, lobsters and Donald Duck: Pennsylvania most gerrymandered districts," PennLive.com, Sept. 27, 2017 https://www.pennlive.com/politics/2017/09/pennsylvania_gerrymandering_di.html

Solution 8: Cut Defense Spending

1 Dwight D. Eisenhower, "Chance for Peace" speech, delivered to the American Society of Newspaper Editors on April 16, 1953 after the death of Joseph Stalin, transcript available through Social Justice Speeches http://www.edchange.org/multicultural/speeches/ike_chance_for_peace.html

2 Fiscal Year 2021 Budget Request Overview, Office of the Under Secretary of Defense, February 2020 https://comptroller.defense.gov/Portals/45/Documents/defbudget/fy2021/fy2021_Budget_Request_Overview_Book.pdf, chapter 1, page 3 and chapter 6, page 1

3 VA 2021 Budget Request: Fast Facts, Department of Veterans Affairs, https://www.va.gov/budget/docs/summary/fy2021VAsBudgetFastFacts.pdf

4 FY 2021 Budget in Brief," Department of Homeland Security https://www.dhs.gov/sites/default/files/publications/fy_2021_dhs_bib_web_version.pdf

5 "Overview of FY 2020 Appropriations for Commerce, Justice, Science and Related Agencies," Congressional Research Service, Jan. 29, 2020 https://fas.org/sgp/crs/misc/R45702.pdf

6 "FY 2021 Presidential Budget for NNSA Released," National Nuclear Security Administration, Feb. 10, 2020 https://www.energy.gov/nnsa/articles/fy-2021-presidential-budget-nnsa-released

7 Mieke Eoyang and Matt Bennett, Third Way, "Preserving Security by Curbing Pentagon Spending," The Hill blogs, Dec. 13, 2012https://thehill.com/blogs/congress-blog/economy-a-budget/272573-preserving-security-by-curbing-pentagon-spending

8 https://www.worldometers.info/world-population/us-population/

9 "World military expenditure grows to $1.8 trillion in 2018," Stockholm International Peace Research Institute, April 20, 2019 https://www.sipri.org/media/press-release/2019/world-military-expenditure-grows-18-trillion-2018

10 Jim Arkedis, "Time to End Supplemental Budgeting," Progressive Policy Institute, June 30, 2010 https://www.progressivepolicy.org/blog/time-to-end-supplemental-budgeting/

11 Medea Benjamin, John Tierney, David Vine and Col. (Ret.) Lawrence Wilkerson, "Military spending has many points of contention: Closing overseas bases isn't one of them," The Hill, July 17, 2019 https://thehill.com/opinion/national-security/453486-military-spending-has-many-points-of-contention-closing-overseas

12 Julian Barnes, "Lockheed Lobbies for F-22 Production on Job Grounds, The Los Angeles Times, Feb. 11, 2009 https://www.latimes.com/archives/la-xpm-2009-feb-11-fi-jets11-story.html; "Lockheed Martin F-22 Raptor," Wikipedia https://en.wikipedia.org/wiki/Lockheed_Martin_F-22_Raptor

13 Niv M. Sultan, "Defense sector contributions locked in on committee members," OpenSecrets.org, March 2, 2017 https://www.opensecrets.org/news/2017/03/defense-sector-contributions/

14 Laura Litvan and Julie Bykowicz, "Defense-Cut Hypocrisy Makes GOP Converge with Democrats," *Bloomberg Business News*, Feb. 19, 2013 https://www.bloomberg.com/news/articles/2013-02-20/defense-cut-hypocrisy-makes-gop-converge-with-democrats?sref=zcBXJvHi

15 Aaron Mehta and Lydia Mulvany, "The Army Tank That Could Not Be Stopped," The Center for Public Integrity, July 30, 2012, updated May 19, 2014 https://publicintegrity.org/national-security/the-army-tank-that-could-not-be-stopped/

16 Kathleen Miller, Tony Capaccio and Danielle Ivory, "Flawed F-35 Too Big to Kill as Lockheed Hooks 45 States," *Bloomberg Business News*, Feb. 22, 2013 https://www.bloomberg.com/news/articles/2013-02-22/flawed-f-35-fighter-too-big-to-kill-as-lockheed-hooks-45-states?sref=zcBXJvHi

17 Anthony Capaccio, "Navy's New $7.8 Billion Destroyer Is Now Running Six Years Late," *Bloomberg News*, Oct. 9, 2019 https://www.bloomberg.com/news/articles/2019-10-09/navy-s-new-7-8-billion-destroyer-is-now-running-six-years-late?sref=zcBXJvHi

18 "Defense Budget Overview," Page 2-4, U.S. Department of Defense, Feb. 2020 https://comptroller.defense.gov/Portals/45/Documents/defbudget/fy2021/fy2021_Budget_Request_Overview_Book.pdf and "Budget Authority in the Department of Defense's Base Budget," Congressional Budget Office, 2014 https://www.cbo.gov/sites/default/files/49764-Land-Table1.jpg

19 Costs of War," Watson Institute of International and Public Affairs, Brown University, Nov. 13, 2019 https://watson.brown.edu/costsofwar/figures/2019/budgetary-costs-post-911-wars-through-fy2020-64-trillion and "Human Costs," Watson Institute, January 2020 https://watson.brown.edu/costsofwar/costs/human; and Matthew Pennington, Associated Press, "Pentagon says war in Afghanistan costs taxpayers $45 billion per year," *PBS News Hour*, Feb. 6, 2018 https://www.pbs.org/newshour/politics/pentagon-says-afghan-war-costs-taxpayers-45-billion-per-year

20 Compiled from Wikipedia list https://en.wikipedia.org/wiki/List_of_active_United_States_military_aircraft and Modern Airpower 2020 https://www.militaryfactory.com/modern-airpower/index.asp

21 "Aircraft carriers by country 2020," World Population Review http://worldpopulationreview.com/countries/aircraft-carriers-by-country/; "USS Gerald Ford (computer model)", CNET, Dec. 10, 2019 https://www.cnet.com/pictures/meet-the-navys-new-13-billion-aircraft-carrier/10/ and Kyle Mizokami, "The Navy's Newest Aircraft Carrier Is Delayed, Yet Again," Popular Mechanics, March 28, 2019 https://www.popularmechanics.com/military/navy-ships/a26975852/the-navys-newest-aircraft-carrier-is-delayed-yet-again/

22 Caleb Larson, "America's Strong Marine Corps Is Only One Of The World's Best Fighting Forces," Center for the National Interest, Jan. 22, 2020 https://nationalinterest.org/blog/buzz/americas-strong-marine-corps-only-one-worlds-best-fighting-forces-116291; and "Strength of British military falls for ninth year," BBC News, Aug. 16, 2019 https://www.bbc.com/news/uk-49365599

23 Kelsey Reichmann, "Here's how many nuclear warheads exist, and which countries own them," Defense News, June 16, 2019 https://www.defensenews.com/global/2019/06/16/heres-how-many-nuclear-warheads-exist-and-which-countries-own-them/

24 Neta C. Crawford, "Drones Are Cheap. A War With Iran Isn't." Barron's, Jan. 3, 2020 https://www.barrons.com/articles/drones-are-cheap-a-war-with-iran-isnt-51578091713

25 "Costs of War," Watson Institute of International and Public Affairs, Brown University, Nov. 13, 2019 https://watson.brown.edu/costsofwar/figures/2019/budgetary-costs-post-911-wars-through-fy2020-64-trillion and "Human Costs," Watson Institute, January 2020 https://watson.brown.edu/costsofwar/costs/human

26 Dwight D. Eisenhower, "1961 Farewell Address," National Archives, Dwight D. Eisenhower Presidential Library, available at https://www.ourdocuments.gov/doc.php?flash=false&doc=90&page=transcript

Solution 9: Return to a Responsible Foreign Policy

1 Jeane Kirkpatrick, "Legitimacy and Force, Volume 2, National and International Dimensions," published by Transaction Books, 1988. https://books.google.com/books?id=gEymDLmOuOgC&pg=PA6-IA16&lpg=PA6-IA16&dq=%E2%80%9CWords+can+destroy.+What+we+call+each+other+ultimately+becomes+what+we+think+of+each+other,+and+it+matters.%E2%80%9D+%E2%80%94Jeane+Kirkpatrick,&source=bl&ots=iBlfgwXrZM&sig=ACfU3U2VZfhNwL94-XrEibu2f3mCvSoK8w&hl=en&sa=X&ved=2ahUKEwi7zLv2mcPnAhXJKMOKHSNNBdoQ6AEwDnoECAoQAQ#v=onepage&q=%E2%80%9CWords%20can%20destroy.%20What%20we%20call%20each%20other%20ultimately%20becomes%20what%20we%20think%20of%20each%20other%2C%20and%20it%20matters.%E2%80%9D%20%E2%80%94Jeane%20Kirkpatrick%2C&f=false

2 Our Mission Statement," U.S. Department of State, May 10, 2010 https://2009-2017.state.gov/s/d/rm/rls/perfrpt/2009performancesummary/html/139613.htm

3 "Exports of goods and services (% of GDP)—United States," The World Bank, 2019 https://data.worldbank.org/indicator/NE.EXP.GNFS.ZS?locations=US:

4 "Exports of goods and services (% of GDP)—United States," The World Bank, 2019 https://data.worldbank.org/indicator/NE.EXP.GNFS.ZS?locations=US

5 "U.S. Trade in Goods and Services—Balance of Payments Basis," U.S. Census Bureau, Economic Analysis Division, Feb. 5, 2020 https://www.census.gov/foreign-trade/statistics/historical/gands.pdf

6 U.S. Bureau of Economic Analysis and the Census Bureau. https://www.bea.gov/system/files/2020-02/trad1219annual-fax.pdf

7 David Brooks, "Voters, Your Foreign Policy Views Stink," *The New York Times*, June 13, 2019 https://www.nytimes.com/2019/06/13/opinion/foreign-policy-populism.html

8 John McCain, as reported on CNN, Aug. 27, 2018 https://www.cnn.com/2018/08/27/politics/john-mccain-farewell-statement/index.html

9 David E. Sanger and Catie Edmondson, "Russia Targeted Election Systems in All 50 States, Report Finds," *The New York Times*, July 25, 2019 https://www.nytimes.com/2019/07/25/us/politics/russian-hacking-elections.html

10 Neta C. Crawford, "Costs of War—United States Budgetary Costs of the Post-9/11 Wars Through FY2019: $5.9 Trillion Spent and Obligated," Brown University, Watson Institute, Nov. 14, 2018 https://watson.brown.edu/costsofwar/files/cow/imce/papers/2018/Crawford_Costs%20of%20War%20Estimates%20Through%20FY2019.pdf

11 Jim Mattis and Bing West, "Call Sign Chaos: Learning to Lead," published by Random House, Sept. 3, 2019

12 "Level Peace Corps Funding Approved for FY2020," National Peace Corps Association, Dec. 17, 2019 https://www.peacecorpsconnect.org/articles/congress-set-to-approve-level-peace-corps-funding#:~:text=After%20weeks%20of%20negotiations%2C%2 Congress,%24410.5%20million%20for%20Peace%20Corps

13 Thomas L. Friedman, "Thank You for Being Late: An Optimist's Guide to Thriving in the Age of Accelerations," published by Farrar, Straus and Giroux, Nov. 22, 2016

14 Thomas L. Friedman, "Tanks, Jets or Scholarships?", *The New York Times*, May 1, 2012 https://www.nytimes.com/2012/05/02/opinion/friedman-tanks-jets-or-scholarships.html

Solution 10: Reduce Gun Deaths in America

1   Cameron Kasky, "Parkland student: My generation won't stand for this," *CNN Opinion*, Feb. 20, 2018 https://www.cnn.com/2018/02/15/opinions/florida-shooting-no-more-opinion-kasky/index.html

2   John Gramlich, "What the data says about gun deaths in the U.S.," Pew Research Center FactTank, Aug. 16, 2019 https://www.pewresearch.org/fact-tank/2019/08/16/what-the-data-says-about-gun-deaths-in-the-u-s/

3   John Gramlich, "What the data says about gun deaths in the U.S.," Pew Research Center FactTank, Aug. 16, 2019 https://www.pewresearch.org/fact-tank/2019/08/16/what-the-data-says-about-gun-deaths-in-the-u-s/

4   John Gramlich, "What the data says about gun deaths in the U.S.," Pew Research Center FactTank, Aug. 16, 2019 https://www.pewresearch.org/fact-tank/2019/08/16/what-the-data-says-about-gun-deaths-in-the-u-s/

5   Nurith Aizenman and Marc Silver, "How the U.S. Compares With Other Countries in Deaths from Gun Violence," NPR, Aug. 5, 2019 https://www.npr.org/sections/goatsandsoda/2019/08/05/743579605/how-the-u-s-compares-to-other-countries-in-deaths-from-gun-violence

6   "Everytown for Gun Safety Releases New Report on Gun Violence in America as Gun Violence Survivors Week Begins," Everytown for Gun Safety, Feb. 1, 2019 https://everytown.org/press/everytown-for-gun-safety-releases-new-report-on-gun-violence-in-america-as-gun-violence-survivors-week-begins/

7   Compiled from annual data from Centers for Disease Control and Giffords Law Center to Prevent Gun Violence.

8   Pew Research Center FactTank, Aug. 16, 2019 https://www.pewresearch.org/fact-tank/2019/08/16/what-the-data-says-about-gun-deaths-in-the-u-s/

9   Fareed Zakaria, "The Solution to Gun Violence is Clear," *The Washington Post*, Dec. 19, 2012 https://www.washingtonpost.com/opinions/fareed-zakaria-the-solution-to-gun-violence-is-clear/2012/12/19/110a6f82-4a15-11e2-b6f0-e851e741d196_story.html

10   Mark Follman, Julia Lurie, Jaeah Lee and James West, "The True Cost of Gun Violence in America," Mother Jones, April 15, 2015 https://www.motherjones.com/politics/2015/04/true-cost-of-gun-violence-in-america/

11   Dana Bash, "'Stronger, better, tougher:' Giffords improves but she'll never be the same," CNN News, April 10, 2013 https://www.cnn.com/2013/04/09/politics/giffords-health/index.html

12   Christopher Ingraham, "Shooting in Oregon: So far in 2015, we've had 274 days and 294 mass shootings," *The Washington Post*, Oct. 1, 2015 https://www.washingtonpost.com/news/wonk/wp/2015/10/01/2015-274-days-294-mass-shootings-hundreds-dead/

13   https://www.gunviolencearchive.org/reports/mass-shooting?year=2019

14   Ezra Klein, "Twelve facts about guns and mass shootings in the United States," *The Washington Post*, Dec. 14, 2012 https://www.washingtonpost.com/news/wonk/wp/2012/12/14/nine-facts-about-guns-and-mass-shootings-in-the-united-states/

15   "From a 1991 interview on PBS's "MacNeil/Lehrer NewsHour" and quoted in several articles, including Nina Totenberg, "From 'Fraud' to Individual Right, Where Does the Supreme Court Stand on Guns?" National Public Radio, March 5, 2018 https://www.npr.org/2018/03/05/590920670/from-fraud-to-individual-right-where-does-the-supreme-court-stand-on-guns; also available on video at https://www.youtube.com/watch?v=Eya_k4P-iEo

16   Mike DeBonis and Emily Guskin, "Americans of both parties overwhelmingly support 'red flag' laws, expanded background checks for gun buyers, *Washington Post*-ABC News poll finds," *The Washington Post*, Sept. 9, 2019 https://www.washingtonpost.com/politics/americans-of-both-parties-overwhelmingly-support-red-flag-laws-expanded-gun-background-checks-washington-post-abc-news-poll-finds/2019/09/08/97208916-ca75-11e9-a4f3-c081a126de70_story.html; Kenneth T. Walsh, "Poll: Majority Favor Gun Control," *U.S. News and World Report*, Aug. 19, 2019 https://www.usnews.com/news/national-news/articles/2019-08-19/poll-majority-favor-gun-control; and Domenico Montanaro, "Americans Largely Support Gun Restrictions To 'Do Something' About Gun Violence," National Public Radio, Aug. 10, 2019 https://www.npr.org/2019/08/10/749792493/americans-largely-support-gun-restrictions-to-do-something-about-gun-violence

17 Sari Horwitz, "Glock semiautomatic pistol links recent mass shootings," *The Washington Post*, July 20, 2012 https://www.washingtonpost.com/national/glock-semiautomatic-pistol-links-recent-mass-shootings/2012/07/20/gJQAINYwyW_story.html

18 Matt Gutman and Bill Hutchinson, "Gun law loophole allowed Odessa mass shooting suspect to buy AR-type assault rifle: Sources," *ABC News*, Sept. 3, 2019, https://abcnews.go.com/US/gun-loophole-allowed-west-texas-mass-shooting-suspect/story?id=65363861

19 Bill Chappell, "The Pistol That Looks Like a Rifle: The Dayton Shooter's Gun," *National Public Radio*, Aug. 8, 2019 https://www.npr.org/2019/08/08/748665339/the-pistol-that-looks-like-a-rifle-the-dayton-shooters-gun

20 Jolie McCullough, "El Paso shooting suspect said he ordered his AK-47 and ammo from overseas," *The Texas Tribune*, Aug. 28, 2019 https://www.texastribune.org/2019/08/28/el-paso-shooting-gun-romania/

21 Ryan Sabalow, "What we know about the gun used in the Gilroy Garlic Festival shooting," *The Sacramento Bee*, July 29, 2019 https://www.sacbee.com/news/california/article233266349.html

22 David K. Li, "California bar shooting: Gun used was a Glock 21 .45-caliber handgun," *NBC News*, Nov. 8, 2018 https://www.nbcnews.com/news/us-news/gun-used-thousand-oaks-bar-shooting-was-glock-21-45-n933976

23 Richard A. Oppel, Jr. "Synagogue Suspect's Guns Were All Purchased Legally, Inquiry Finds," *The New York Times*, Oct. 30, 2018 https://www.nytimes.com/2018/10/30/us/ar15-gun-pittsburgh-shooting.html

24 Alex Horton, "The Las Vegas shooter modified a dozen rifles to shoot like automatic weapons," *The Washington Post,* Oct. 3, 2017 https://www.washingtonpost.com/news/checkpoint/wp/2017/10/02/video-from-las-vegas-suggests-automatic-gunfire-heres-what-makes-machine-guns-different/

25 Fareed Zakaria, "The Solution to Gun Violence is Clear," *The Washington Post*, Dec. 19, 2012 https://www.washingtonpost.com/opinions/fareed-zakaria-the-solution-to-gun-violence-is-clear/2012/12/19/110a6f82-4a15-11e2-b6f0-e851e741d196_story.html

26 Giffords Law Center to Prevent Gun Violence: https://lawcenter.giffords.org/gun-laws/policy-areas/background-checks/universal-background-checks/

27 Giffords Law Center to Prevent Gun Violence: https://lawcenter.giffords.org gun-laws/policy-areas/background-checks/universal-background-checks/

28 Theresa Waldrop, "West Texas shooter bought gun in private sale," CNN News, Sept. 3, 2019 https://www.cnn.com/2019/09/03/us/west-texas-shooter-gun/index.html

29 Jeanne Marie Laskas, "Inside the Federal Bureau of Way Too Many Guns," GQ, Aug. 30, 2016 https://www.gq.com/story/inside-federal-bureau-of-way-too-many-guns

30 Mike Baker, "Setting Sights on the AR-15: After Las Vegas Shooting, Lawyers Target Gun Companies," *The New York Times*, July 3, 2019 https://www.nytimes.com/2019/07/03/us/bumpstocks-las-vegas-guns-manufacturers-lawsuit.html

Solution 11: Fix the Legal System

1 Lewis F. Powell, Jr., as quoted in numerous books and publications, including on the University of Virginia School of Law website https://www.law.virginia.edu/public-service/powell-fellowship-legal-services

2 Drew Kann, "Five facts behind America's high incarceration rate," CNN News, April 21, 2019 https://www.cnn.com/2018/06/28/us/mass-incarceration-five-key-facts/index.html

3 Jeff Jacoby, "U.S. legal bubble can't pop soon enough," Boston Globe, May 9, 2014 https://www.bostonglobe.com/opinion/2014/05/09/the-lawyer-bubble-pops-not-moment-too-soon/qAYzQ823qpfi4GQl2OiPZM/story.html

4 Jeff Jacoby, "U.S. legal bubble can't pop soon enough," Boston Globe, May 9, 2014 https://www.bostonglobe.com/opinion/2014/05/09/the-lawyer-bubble-pops-not-moment-too-soon/qAYzQ823qpfi4GQl2OiPZM/story.html

5 J. Mark Ramseyer and Eric B. Rasmusen, "Comparative Litigation Rates," Harvard University, John M. Olin Center for Law, Economics and Business, November 2010 http://www.law.harvard.edu/programs/olin_center/papers/pdf/Ramseyer_681.pdf

6 "Membership of the 116th Congress: A Profile," Congressional Research Service, Jan. 14, 2020 https://fas.org/sgp/crs/misc/R45583.pdf

7 Adam Liptak, "U.S. prison population dwarfs that of other nations," *The New York Times*, April 23, 2008 https://www.nytimes.com/2008/04/23/world/americas/23iht-23prison.12253738.html

8 "World Prison Brief Data," 2020 https://www.prisonstudies.org/world-prison-brief-data

9 Melissa S. Kearney, Benjamin H. Harris, Elisa Jácome, and Lucie Parker, "Ten Economic Facts About Crime and Incarceration in the United States," The Hamilton Project, May 2014 https://www.hamiltonproject.org/assets/legacy/files/downloads_and_links/v8_THP_10CrimeFacts.pdf

10 Melissa S. Kearney, "The Economic Challenges of Crime & Incarceration in the United States," The Hamilton Project, Brookings Institution, Dec. 22, 2014 https://www.hamiltonproject.org/blog/the_economic_challenges_of_crime_incarceration_in_the_united_states

11 "World Prison Brief Data," 2020 https://www.prisonstudies.org/world-prison-brief-data

12 Wendy Sawyer and Peter Wagner, "Mass Incarceration: The Whole Pie 2019," Prison Policy Initiative, March 19, 2019 https://www.prisonpolicy.org/reports/pie2019.html

13 "ACLU Lawsuit Goes After $2 Billion Bail Industry That Profits Off Poor People," American Civil Liberties Union, April 17, 2019 https://www.aclu.org/press-releases/aclu-lawsuit-goes-after-2-billion-bail-industry-profits-poor-people

14 Eve Tushnet, "Fifteen to Life: 15 Ways to Fix the Criminal Justice System," Crisis Magazine, March 1, 2003 https://www.crisismagazine.com/2003/fifteen-to-life-15-ways-to-fix-the-criminal-justice-system

15 Eve Tushnet, "Fifteen to Life: 15 Ways to Fix the Criminal Justice System," Crisis Magazine, March 1, 2003 https://www.crisismagazine.com/2003/fifteen-to-life-15-ways-to-fix-the-criminal-justice-system

16 Morris Hoffman, "A Judge on the Injustice of America's Extreme Prison Sentences," *The Wall Street Journal*, Feb. 7, 2019 https://www.wsj.com/articles/a-judge-on-the-injustice-of-americas-extreme-prison-sentences-11549557185

Solution 12: Embrace the Immigration Advantage

1 Madeleine Albright, "Immigration Reform," Congressional Record Volume 160, Number 48, March 26, 2014 https://www.govinfo.gov/content/pkg/CREC-2014-03-26/html/CREC-2014-03-26-pt1-PgH2652.htm

2 Ronald Reagan, "Reagan's Statement on Immigration," *The New York Times*, July 31, 1981 https://www.nytimes.com/1981/07/31/us/reagan-s-statement-on-immigration.html

3 Carol Morello, "U.S. surpasses Syrian refugee goal set by Obama, expects more next year," *The Washington Post*, Sept. 27, 2016 https://www.washingtonpost.com/world/national-security/us-surpasses-syrian-refugee-goal-set-by-obama-expects-more-next-year/2016/09/27/59cedeb8-84e7-11e6-ac72-a29979381495_story.html

4 Nicholas Kristof, "Canada, Leading the Free World," *The New York Times*, Feb. 4, 2017 https://www.nytimes.com/2017/02/04/opinion/sunday/canada-leading-the-free-world.html

5 Nicholas Kristof, "Canada, Leading the Free World," *The New York Times*, Feb. 4, 2017 https://www.nytimes.com/2017/02/04/opinion/sunday/canada-leading-the-free-world.html

6 Linda Qiu, "Border Crossings Have Been Declining for Years, Despite Claims of a 'Crisis in Illegal Immigration,'" *The New York Times*, June 20, 2018 https://www.nytimes.com/2018/06/20/us/politics/fact-check-trump-border-crossings-declining-.html

7   Bill Chappell, "U.S. Births Fell to a 32-Year Low in 2018: CDC Says Birthrate is in Record Slump," National Public Radio, May 15, 2019 https://www.npr.org/2019/05/15/723518379/u-s-births-fell-to-a-32-year-low-in-2018-cdc-says-birthrate-is-at-record-level

8   Ben Gitis and Jacqueline Varas, "The Labor and Output Declines from Removing All Undocumented Immigrants," American Action Forum, May 5, 2016 https://www.americanactionforum.org/research/labor-output-declines-removing-undocumented-immigrants/

9   Dustin McKissen, "This Study Immigrants are Far More Likely to Start New Businesses Than Native-Born Americans," Inc., Feb. 21, 2017 https://www.inc.com/dustin-mckissen/study-shows-immigrants-are-more-than-twice-as-likely-to-become-entrepreneurs.html

10   Jynnah Radford, "Key findings about U.S. immigrants," Pew Research Center FactTanks, June 17, 2019 https://www.pewresearch.org/fact-tank/2019/06/17/key-findings-about-u-s-immigrants/

11   Stuart Anderson, "55% of America's Billion-Dollar Startups Have an Immigrant Founder," *Forbes* magazine, Oct. 25, 2018 https://www.forbes.com/sites/stuartanderson/2018/10/25/55-of-americas-billion-dollar-startups-have-immigrant-founder/#76911f6748ee

12   President George W. Bush, speech on immigration on May 15, 2006—transcript available at *The New York Times* https://www.nytimes.com/2006/05/15/washington/15text-bush.html

13   Ananya Bhattacharya, "One of Amazon's fiercest competitors in India was created by an H-1B reject," Quartz India, Feb. 6, 2017 https://qz.com/india/903861/one-of-amazons-fiercest-competitors-in-india-was-created-by-an-h-1b-reject/

14   Jynnah Radford, "Key Findings About U.S. Immigrants," Pew Research Center FactTank, June 17, 2019 https://www.pewresearch.org/fact-tank/2019/06/17/key-findings-about-u-s-immigrants/

Solution 13: Save Social Security

1   Jon Meacham, "Need to Know," *PBS*, Jan. 27, 2012 https://www.pbs.org/wnet/need-to-know/video/american-voices-jon-meacham-on-our-obligation-to-the-elderly/12976/

2   Excerpts from a speech by Frank Bane, "Problems of Social Security," America's Town Meeting of the Air, Dec. 10, 1936 https://www.ssa.gov/history/banesp.html

3   Kathleen Romig, "Social Security Lifts More Americans Above Poverty Than Any Other Program," Center on Budget and Policy Priorities, July 19, 2019 https://www.cbpp.org/research/social-security/social-security-lifts-more-americans-above-poverty-than-any-other-program

4   Kathleen Romig, "Social Security Lifts More Americans Above Poverty Than Any Other Program," Center on Budget and Policy Priorities, July 19, 2019 https://www.cbpp.org/research/social-security/social-security-lifts-more-americans-above-poverty-than-any-other-program

5   Editorial board, "Social Security, Present and Future," *The New York Times*, March 30, 2013 https://www.nytimes.com/2013/03/31/opinion/sunday/social-security-present-and-future.html

6   "Policy Basics: Top Ten Facts about Social Security," Center on Budget and Policy Priorities, Aug. 14, 2019 https://www.cbpp.org/research/social-security/policy-basics-top-ten-facts-about-social-security

7   "Status of the Social Security and Medicare Programs—A Summary of the 2019 Annual Reports," Social Security Administration, https://www.ssa.gov/OACT/TRSUM/index.html

8   "Fact Sheet: Social Security," Social Security Administration https://www.ssa.gov/news/press/factsheets/basicfact-alt.pdf

9   "Life Expectancy for Social Security," Social Security Administration https://www.ssa.gov/history/lifeexpect.html

10 Jiaquan Xu, M.D., Sherry L. Murphy, B.S., Kenneth D. Kochanek, M.A., and Elizabeth Arias, Ph.D. "Mortality in the United States: 2018," National Center for Health Statistics, January 2020 https://www.cdc.gov/nchs/data/databriefs/db355-h.pdf

11 "Fast Facts and Figures about Social Security 2018 — Earnings in Covered Employment, 1937-2017" Social Security Administration https://www.ssa.gov/policy/docs/chartbooks/fast_facts/2018/fast_facts18.html

12 Gretchen Livingston, "Is U.S. fertility at an all-time low? Two of three measures point to yes," Pew Research Center FactTank, May 22, 2019https://www.pewresearch.org/fact-tank/

13 Emily Brandon, "Five Potential Social Security Fixes," U.S. News & World Report, Nov. 14, 2014 https://money.usnews.com/money/blogs/planning-to-retire/2014/11/14/5-potential-social-security-fixes

14 "Raise the Full Retirement Age for Social Security," Congressional Budget Office, Dec. 13, 2018 https://www.cbo.gov/budget-options/2018/54745

15 Steve Kroft (produced by James Jacoby and Michael Karzis), "Disability, USA," 60 Minutes, Oct. 10, 2013 https://www.cbsnews.com/news/disability-usa/

16 Steve Kroft (produced by James Jacoby and Michael Karzis), "Disability, USA," 60 Minutes, Oct. 10, 2013 https://www.cbsnews.com/news/disability-usa/

Solution 14: Simplify the Tax Code

1   Albert Einstein, quoted in "Tax Quotes," Internal Revenue Service
    https://www.irs.gov/newsroom/tax-quotes

2   John McClelland and Jeffrey Werling, "How the 2017 Tax Act Affects CBO's
    projections," Congressional Budget Office, April 20, 2018 https://www.cbo.gov/
    publication/53787; Huaqun Li and Kyle Pomerleau, "The Distributional Impact of
    the Tax Cuts and Jobs Act Over the Next Decade," Tax Foundation, June 18, 2018
    https://taxfoundation.org/the-distributional-impact-of-the-tax-cuts-and-jobs-
    act-over-the-next-decade/

3   Andrew Soergel, "Republicans Circulate Final Draft of Tax Plan," U.S. News
    & World Report, Dec. 15, 2017 https://www.usnews.com/news/economy/
    articles/2017-12-15/estate-tax-student-loan-deductions-stick-around-in-gops-
    final-tax-plan

4   Ben Casselman and Jim Tankersley, "Face It: You (Probably) Got a Tax Cut,"
    The New York Times, April 14, 2019 https://www.nytimes.com/2019/04/14/
    business/economy/income-tax-cut.html

5   John Hamilton, "No city would ever pass this tax bill," The Washington Post,
    Dec. 7, 2017 https://www.washingtonpost.com/opinions/no-city-would-ever-
    pass-this-tax-bill/2017/12/07/899216ac-dad5-11e7-b859-fb0995360725_story.
    html

6   Christopher Ingraham, "For the first time in history, U.S. billionaires paid a lower
    tax rate than the working class last year," The Washington Post, Oct. 8, 2019
    https://www.washingtonpost.com/business/2019/10/08/first-time-history-us-
    billionaires-paid-lower-tax-rate-than-working-class-last-year/; Emmanuel Saez
    and Gabriel Zucman, The Triumph of Injustice: How the Rich Dodge Taxes and
    How to Make Them Pay, published by W.W. Norton & Company, Oct. 15, 2019

7   Christopher Ingraham, "For the first time in history, U.S. billionaires paid a lower
    tax rate than the working class last year," The Washington Post, Oct. 8, 2019
    https://www.washingtonpost.com/business/2019/10/08/first-time-history-us-
    billionaires-paid-lower-tax-rate-than-working-class-last-year/; Emmanuel Saez
    and Gabriel Zucman, The Triumph of Injustice: How the Rich Dodge Taxes and
    How to Make Them Pay, published by W.W. Norton & Company, Oct. 15, 2019

8   "Back to School statistics," Fast Fact, National Center for Education Statistics,
    Institute of Education Sciences, 2019 https://nces.ed.gov/fastfacts/display.
    asp?id=372

9   Oliver Wendell Holmes, Jr., quoted in numerous sources, including "Maintain
    Your Quality of Life in Retirement," Thorson Financial Estate Management
    https://www.thorsonfinancial.com/unbiased-free-advice-services/income-
    tax-reduction-ideas/

10 Jason Russell, "Look at how many pages are in the federal tax code," Washington Examiner, April 15, 2016, with references to Wolters Kluwer. https://www.washingtonexaminer.com/look-at-how-many-pages-are-in-the-federal-tax-code

11 John McCormack, "GE Filed 57,000-page Tax Return, Paid No Taxes on $14 Billion in Profits," Washington Examiner, Nov. 17, 2011 https://www.washingtonexaminer.com/weekly-standard/ge-filed-57-000-page-tax-return-paid-no-taxes-on-14-billion-in-profits

12 "Offshore Shell Games 2017," Institute on Taxation and Economic Policy, Oct. 17, 2017 https://itep.org/offshoreshellgames2017/

13 Offshore Shell Games 2017," Institute on Taxation and Economic Policy, Oct. 17, 2017 https://itep.org/offshoreshellgames2017/

14 Offshore Shell Games 2017," Institute on Taxation and Economic Policy, Oct. 17, 2017 https://itep.org/offshoreshellgames2017/

15 Alex Webb and Mark Gurman, "Apple, Returning Overseas Cash, to Pay $38 Billion Tax Bill," Bloomberg News, Jan. 17, 2018 https://www.bloomberg.com/news/articles/2018-01-17/apple-expects-38-billion-tax-bill-on-overseas-repatriated-cash

16 Reade Pickert, "U.S. Companies' Repatriated Cash Hits $1 Trillion Under Tax Law," Bloomberg News, Dec. 19, 2019 https://www.bloomberg.com/news/articles/2019-12-19/u-s-companies-repatriated-cash-hits-1-trillion-under-tax-law?sref=zcBXJvHi

17 Adam Kazda, "The more complex the tax code, the more the wealthy benefit," The Hill, July 25, 2017 https://thehill.com/blogs/pundits-blog/economy-budget/343645-the-more-complex-the-tax-code-the-more-the-rich-benefit

18 Nina Olson, National Taxpayer Advocate, reported in Ellen Kant, "A Stark Reminder of the Excessive Cost of Complying with the Tax Code," Tax Foundation, Jan. 15, 2013 https://taxfoundation.org/stark-reminder-excessive-cost-complying-tax-code/

19 Nina Olson, National Taxpayer Advocate, reported in Ellen Kant, "A Stark Reminder of the Excessive Cost of Complying with the Tax Code," Tax Foundation, Jan. 15, 2013 https://taxfoundation.org/stark-reminder-excessive-cost-complying-tax-code/

20 Josh Dzieza, "8 Ridiculous Tax Loopholes: How Companies are Avoiding the Tax Man," Daily Beast, published Feb. 25, 2012 and updated July 13, 2017 https://www.thedailybeast.com/8-ridiculous-tax-loopholes-how-companies-are-avoiding-the-tax-man

21 Robert W. Wood, "20 Really Stupid Things in the U.S. Tax Code," Forbes, Dec. 16, 2014 https://www.forbes.com/sites/robertwood/2014/12/16/20-really-stupid-things-in-the-u-s-tax-code/#ae88abb14b60

22 Robert W. Wood, "20 Really Stupid Things in the U.S. Tax Code," *Forbes*, Dec. 16, 2014 https://www.forbes.com/sites/robertwood/2014/12/16/20-really-stupid-things-in-the-u-s-tax-code/#ae88abb14b60

23 "60 Fortune 500 Companies Avoided All Federal Income Tax in 2018 Under New Tax Law," Institute on Taxation and Economic Policy, April 11, 2019 https://itep.org/60-fortune-500-companies-avoided-all-federal-income-tax-in-2018-under-new-tax-law/#:~:text=An%20in%2Ddepth%20analysis%20of,and%20Economic%20Policy%20said%20today.

24 Jay MacDonald, "Five tax deductions that favor the rich," Bankrate, Dec. 7, 2011 https://www.bankrate.com/finance/taxes/tax-deductions-favor-rich-1.aspx

25 Dylan Matthews, "The Republican tax bill got worse: Now the top 1% gets 83% of the gains," Vox, Dec. 18, 2017 https://www.vox.com/policy-and-politics/2017/12/18/16791174/republican-tax-bill-congress-conference-tax-policy-center; and Aimee Picchi, "How much income you need to be in the 1%,"CBS News, Feb. 6, 2019 https://www.cbsnews.com/news/how-much-income-you-need-to-be-in-the-1/

26 "The Bowles-Simpson 'Chairmen's Mark' Deficit Reduction Plan," Tax Policy Center Urban Institute and Brookings Institution, Nov. 12, 2010 https://www.taxpolicycenter.org/taxvox/bowles-simpson-chairmens-mark-deficit-reduction-plan

27 "Jesse Pound," These 91 companies paid no federal taxes in 2018," CNBC, Dec. 16, 2019 https://www.cnbc.com/2019/12/16/these-91-fortune-500-companies-didnt-pay-federal-taxes-in-2018.html

28 Cass Sunstein, "How to Simplify the Tax Code. Simply." TIME USA, May 31, 2013 https://ideas.time.com/2013/05/31/how-to-simplify-the-tax-code-simply/

29 How Could We Improve the Federal Tax System?" Tax Policy Center Briefing Book, Urban Institute and Brookings Institution https://www.taxpolicycenter.org/briefing-book/what-was-experience-california-return-free-tax-filing

30 "How Could We Improve the Federal Tax System?" Tax Policy Center Briefing Book, Urban Institute and Brookings Institution https://www.taxpolicycenter.org/briefing-book/what-other-countries-use-return-free-tax-filing

Solution 15: Reform Campaign Finance

1 Robert W. McChesney, Aug. 26, 2017, quoted on sources that include Daily Quotes Live http://www.dailyquotes.live/tag/robert-mcchesney/

2 Bradley Jones, "Most Americans want to limit campaign spending, say big donors have greater political influence," Pew Research Center FactTank, May 8, 2018 https://www.pewresearch.org/fact-tank/2018/05/08/most-americans-want-to-limit-campaign-spending-say-big-donors-have-greater-political-influence/

3   Jon Schwarz, "Jimmy Carter: The US is an "oligarchy with unlimited political bribery," The Intercept, July 30, 2015, reporting on Jimmy Carter comments on the Thom Hartmann Program radio show. https://theintercept.com/2015/07/30/jimmy-carter-u-s-oligarchy-unlimited-political-bribery/

4   "Did Money Win?" OpenSecrets. Org, Center for Responsive Politics, no publication date listed https://www.opensecrets.org/elections-overview/did-money-win

5   Aliyah Frumin, "How much does it cost to win a seat in Congress? If you have to ask..." MSNBC, March 11, 2013 http://www.msnbc.com/hardball/how-much-does-it-cost-win-seat-congre and Jay Costa, "What's the Cost of a Seat in Congress?" MapLight, March 10, 2013 https://maplight.org/story/whats-the-cost-of-a-seat-in-congress/

6   Laura Olson, "How much did Pennsylvania's U.S. Senate race cost?" The Morning Call, Nov. 17, 2016 https://www.mcall.com/news/local/mc-pa-senate-toomey-mcginty-cost-20161117-story.html

7   Niv M. Sultan, "Outside groups spent more than candidates in 27 races, often by huge amounts," OpenSecrets.org, Center for Responsive Politics, Feb. 24, 2017 https://www.opensecrets.org/news/2017/02/outside-groups-spent-more-than-candidates-in-27-races-often-by-huge-amounts/

8   Brett Samuels, "Rick Scott funded three-quarters of his Senate campaign, to tune of $63.6 million," The Hill, Dec. 10, 2018 https://thehill.com/homenews/campaign/420635-rick-scott-funded-three-quarters-of-senate-campaign-to-tune-of-636-million

9   Fredreka Schouten, "A record $5.7 billion was spent on the 2018 elections for Congress," CNN News, Feb. 7, 2019 https://www.cnn.com/2019/02/07/politics/midterm-election-costs-topped-5-7-billion/index.html

10 Robert B. Reich, "The Common Good," published by Knopf, Feb. 20, 2018

11 Anu Narayanswamy, Chris Alcantara and Michelle Ye Hee Lee, "Meet the wealthy donors pouring millions into the 2018 elections," The Washington Post, Oct. 26, 2018 https://www.washingtonpost.com/graphics/2018/politics/superpac-donors-2018/

12 Nick Penniman, speaking at a Washington Center for Internships and Academic Seminars discussion, Jan. 4, 2018; video available via C-SPAN https://www.c-span.org/video/?439250-2/nick-penniman-money-politics

13 Evan Osnos, "The Money Midterms: A Scandal in Slow Motion," The New Yorker, Oct. 22, 2014 https://www.newyorker.com/news/daily-comment/money-midterms-scandal-slow-motion

14 Transcript of video, "Campaign Finance from Watergate to Soft Money and Citizens United," Oct. 19, 2014, available on RetroReport.org https://www.retroreport.org/transcript/the-cost-of-campaigns/

15 "Origins & Development: From the Constitution to the Modern House—Constitutional Qualifications," History, Art & Archives, United States House of Representatives https://history.house.gov/Institution/Origins-Development/Constitutional-Qualifications/

Solution 16: Create an Economy Built to Last

1 Kimberly Amadeo, "Trump and the National Debt," *The Balance*, March 4, 2020 https://www.thebalance.com/trump-plans-to-reduce-national-debt-4114401

2 "World military expenditure grows to $1.8 trillion in 2018," Stockholm International Peace Research Institute, April 29, 2019 https://www.sipri.org/media/press-release/2019/world-military-expenditure-grows-18-trillion-2018

3 "Fact Sheet: Social Security," Social Security Administration https://www.ssa.gov/news/press/factsheets/basicfact-alt.pdf

4 Jim Haddadin, "Senators forging friendships at the dinner table: All-female club gets things done," Fosters.com, a service of Seacoastonline.com, April 21, 2012, updated April 23, 2012 https://www.fosters.com/article/20120421/GJNEWS_01/704219913

Conclusion

1 "Thoughts on the Cause of the Present Discontents 82-83," published in 1770, as noted on Open Culture http://www.openculture.com/2016/03/edmund-burkeon-in-action.html

2 Tom Brokaw, "The Greatest Generation," published by Penguin Random House, May 11, 2004